Digital Signal Processing

A Gentle Introduction with Audio Signal Examples

Stephen B. Morris

Edition 1.5

December 2021

Disclaimer

The contents of this book are for self-directed, personal learning purposes only. The information is not guaranteed for any particular purpose or application. The publisher does not accept any warranties or representations, nor does it accept any liability with respect to the contents or the use of the contents.

Changes in this Revision

Change Details	Revision	Author	Date
More explanation of digital signals up to page 37	1.5	SM	November 10, 2021
Additional content on spectral leakage up to page 48	1.5	SM	November 20, 2021
New chapter on further uses of Octave up to page 89	1.5	SM	November 23, 2021

Table of Contents

Digital Signal Processing 1

A Gentle Introduction with Audio Signal Examples 1

Disclaimer 2

Changes in this Revision 3

Dedication 6

Introduction 7

Citations 9

Chapter 1 What is a signal? 10

   Audio In Nature 10

   Audio and The London Underground Train System 10

   Modern Audio Applications 11

   Other Signal Types 11

   Using digital signals 12

Chapter 2 Creating a signal with Audacity® 13

   Signal Creation with Audacity 14

      So, What Exactly Is Meant by a "Digital" Signal? 15

   DSP 18

   Generating an audio file 18

   Signal Frequency 19

   Breaking the Monotony 20

Chapter 3 Examining Signals In The Frequency Domain 22

   Dog Whistles and Human Hearing 23

   A Feline-Unfriendly Hoover 24

   Frequency Spectrum 24

   A Multi-tone Signal 25

Chapter 4 Filtering Signals 30

Chapter 5 The DSP Process 34

   Signal Import 34

   Review/Listen 34

   Analyze 35

   Modify 37

   Review/Listen 37

   Save and Signal Export 37

Chapter 6 DSP and the Discrete Fourier Transform (DFT) 38

   Spectral Analysis Using the DFT 39

      DFT Windowing 42

   Audacity Note 45

      DFT Analysis Frequencies 45

      The Analysis Frequencies 48

   Spectral Leakage 50

Chapter 7 Adding GNU Octave to the DSP Work Toolkit 53

   Using Octave 56

   Viewing Audio Data In Octave 59

   Generating an Audio File in Octave 61

Chapter 8 Looking a little more deeply into Octave 67

   Octave DSP Uses – Finding Peak Values 67

   Using Octave to view a basic filter response 68

   Basic Octave Sinusoidal Plot 69

Decimation Example...71
A Chirp Signal 72
An Amplitude Modulation (AM) Example 74
Extracting Signal Components Using the DFT 75
Errors to watch out for when using Octave 78
Chapter 9 More Signal Analysis and a DIY Hearing Test 80
Digging into an Audio Signal as part of the DSP Process Pipeline.........................80
A Pre-existing Audio File..80
Exploring the Human Hearing Range..82
Creating a Test Audio File 83
Spectrum Analysis 84
Conclusions 87
Further Reading 88
Index 89

Dedication

Always and ever for Siobhán.

Introduction

Digital signal processing (DSP) is a complex field. As I look at my bookshelf I have ten reference books on the subject of DSP. It's a tough subject to break into. What makes DSP a little unusual is its rather exotic mix of mathematics, engineering, and its broad (and growing) application to so many fields.

One reason why perhaps there is so much interest in DSP is the sheer depth of the subject. DSP encompasses mathematics, physics and computing. For example, you'll often see the case where a given artifact of interest in a time domain signal can be viewed in a limited way only. An example of this is when you try to determine the existence of a given frequency component in a signal. Determining the signal frequency exists may be relatively simple, however, determining the time domain location of that frequency component may be very difficult or impossible. This sounds a little like the Heisenberg Uncertainty Principle and it is but one example of the richness of the DSP discipline.

There are techniques that can help in managing this difficulty, e.g., taking numerous DFTs where the underlying 'signals' overlap in the time domain. This is called the short-time Fourier Transform and analysis of each sub-signal does provide a means to locate time-specific signal information. Many such techniques exist and each one, in its own way, helps in tackling some knotty signal-related problem. I propose a simple DSP process for iteratively solving such problems.

Did you ever wonder how JPEG images can be used to pack so much information into a compressed file? Well, JPEG makes use of DSP techniques. Or how about the area of automatic error correction? Again, error correction such as that used on audio CDs makes use of DSP techniques. The same is true of video technology. Indeed, every time you listen to music on a digital platform, you are inadvertently making extensive use of DSP. The telecommunications industry has used DSP techniques for many years. Every time you use a phone (smart or otherwise), you are also using DSP.

In my research into and work with DSP, I've found most of the books in the field are either very mathematical or they are skewed somewhat in favour of hardware design. It seems to be hard to find a DSP book that explains how to approach this fascinating subject in simple terms using freely-available software tools to explain the main concepts. This is the main reason why I've written this book. To this end, I've used a very popular, open source, audio editing tool as the basis for a DSP laboratory.

It also seems that DSP has, what might be considered, a slightly darker side as well. If you look up jobs in the area of DSP, it's quite common for positions to require security clearance with no option for remote working. Perhaps DSP is widely used in the defence industry. For this reason also, perhaps some knowledge of this field is a good idea.

DSP can be broadly divided into two main areas: signal analysis and signal processing. In signal analysis, a given signal and its attributes are studied but are typically not changed. In signal processing, a signal is both studied and modified.

When I say 'studied', it is likely that software tools are employed to assist in performing the bulk of the studying task - the raw studying is not done by a person. Rather, software tools are used and this allows for a practitioner to draw conclusions about the signal content. In short, skilled practitioners in the field of DSP work in conjunction with signals, systems, software tools, and algorithms. The use of DSP tends to be iterative in nature: study the signal, modify it, study it, etc.

It's no coincidence therefore that DSP processes are a lot like standard agile software development processes. In agile, tasks are typically broken down into manageable chunks and assigned to team members as part of a short well-defined time-boxed mini-project.

Signal processing, in its traditional sense, typically aims to modify a given signal in some way. An example of this is noise reduction or signal extraction from a noisy channel. This type of task generally involves the use of digital filtering. In other words, filtering forms a key part of this type of DSP workflow.

In the book, we'll set up a small 'laboratory' for looking at some real signals (and also synthetic signals). This is useful because you can get to look at the actual structure of a signal, analyze its spectrum, modify it, and then view the results. This approach looks and sounds a little like agile software development and is done in an effort to help with learning about the fascinating field of DSP.

The approach I adopt is to make the book very visual in nature. So, it includes a large amount of screen shots from the tools selected for use. This is deliberate and aims to present the content in as clear a format as possible. In many cases, I also present cases where errors occur, e.g., selecting the wrong user interface options. Again, this is to assist the reader in getting up to speed with the concepts and tools.

I've always found that repetition is a key element of learning. The book presents some concepts that are foundational in the context of DSP work. One is the benefit of changing perspective when looking at signals. I repeat the importance of this throughout the book with a view to reinforcing the message.

Citations

GNU Octave

John W. Eaton, David Bateman, Søren Hauberg, Rik Wehbring (2021).

GNU Octave version 6.2.0 manual: a high-level interactive language for numerical computations.
URL https://octave.org/doc/v6.2.0/

Chapter 1 What is a signal?

A signal is an ordered sequence of numbers that conveys information. There is perhaps an infinite or nearly infinite number of signals in the natural world, e.g., a sequence of temperatures that changes over a period of time, the data from a heartbeat monitor, an audio wave generated from an online radio stream, a list of stock market prices, and so on. In each such signal, there is some variable quantity that changes over time and signals, such as these, are typically referred to as time domain signals.

Audio signals propagate in space and time. This is rather fortunate because it means that sound travels from its source to its destination. As the sound is received, it is decoded by the recipient. This process continues until the sender stops originating the audio signal.

Audio In Nature

Sound has high importance for communications and indeed survival. Across the natural world, different species have adapted and evolved around their audio requirements. For humans, we use a relatively narrow range of frequencies from 20Hz to 20,000Hz. Elephants can hear as low as 14Hz. Surprisingly, cats can hear up to 64,000Hz, even higher than dogs. But, we're all in the cheap seats compared to bats, who can hear up to a staggering 200,000Hz.

There is even debate about whether cats and dogs can hear Wi-Fi. This could be potentially very unpleasant for our domestic companions.

Sound travels at different speeds in different materials. In air, sound travels at about 340 metres per second. So, when someone takes a minute to respond to a question, you know it's not the speed of the medium that's the cause of the delay! Surprisingly, sound travels slowest in gases, i.e., in air. In liquids, such as water, sound travels at the much faster speed of about 1,481 metres per second. However, in solids, sound travels at an impressive speed at 5,120 metres per second in iron. Compared to the speed of sound in air of 340 metres per second, sound travels through diamond at a blistering rate of 12,000 metres per second.

Audio is a very interesting field of study.

Audio and The London Underground Train System

As the world's first underground train system in 1863, the London underground system was designed to reduce street congestion. The trains were initially steam-based locomotives because that was the only available train technology at the time. Only a few years ago and for the first time, the London Underground carried over 1 billion passengers in a single year.

Audio has always played an important role in train systems and in the UK, there is mixed opinion about the recorded announcements. Some people love them while others hate them! Some enthusiasts even record the announcements and post them on social media. I remember hearing some announcements myself and being puzzled about the language, quite apart from understanding the content.

There's a famous London Underground safety announcement that has been in use for many years. It's a registered trademark, so I can't use it here. But, the announcement was the subject of a short film on YouTube – https://www.youtube.com/watch?v=aJNLfGQIZOU.

Modern Audio Applications

Voice recognition products are increasingly common and users are quite comfortable interacting with search engines via voice commands. Other domestic devices also use voice recognition for interactions. This type of application is not with a degree of controversy as there are rumours that the voice commands are pretty much stored in perpetuity.

Other Signal Types

There are other signal types that vary in space rather than time, e.g., a black and white digital image is a two-dimensional grid of numeric values. Each element in the grid represents the smallest part of the overall image. Adding colour to an image adds additional dimension to what can be considered the signal.

In a similar sense, a video signal is a signal composed of a large number of interconnected images that change over time. Video signals can be considered to propagate in two-dimensional space and time. For this reason, the digital storage of video signals can consume an inordinate amount of disk space.

The key point to note is that there are many signals that can be usefully studied.

A foundational distinction must be made between continuous signals and digital signals. Perhaps, the best way to understand the difference between continuous and digital signals is to look at a picture of each one.

Figure 1-1 illustrates, in one diagram, the difference between a continuous signal and a digital signal.

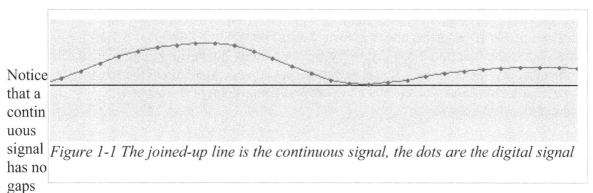

Notice that a continuous signal has no gaps

Figure 1-1 The joined-up line is the continuous signal, the dots are the digital signal

along its contours. In other words, the continuous signal is just that - continuous without any breaks or gaps. Storing a continuous signal in a computer is not really possible because it requires essentially infinite storage.

This issue of infinite storage is an interesting paradox because an example of a continuous signal is the audio encoded on a vinyl record disk. How can a finite object, such as a vinyl disk, hold what seems to be an infinite amount of data? This is a good question and reflects what might be considered the fractal nature of continuous signals. A similar notion applies to the fractal nature of coastal country maps, i.e., the coast is finite and yet in the fractal context, the path can be considered to be infinitely long. Clearly, DSP is an interesting area!

By filling in the gaps between the dots in Figure 1-1, you go from a digital to a continuous signal. Please note that the latter is purely a thought experiment used for illustration – it's not possible to fill in the gaps because the gaps arise as a result of the original analogue-to-digital sampling process. For this reason, in reality, it is the reverse that happens, i.e., we start with a continuous signal which we then sample and digitize. The stream of quantized and digitized samples then forms the basis for the digital signal (or the dots in Figure 1-1).

It's essential to appreciate that the data contained in the gaps is discarded during sampling and is therefore gone forever. It simply doesn't exist and when we listen to such audio, our brain fills in the gaps so that we hear a continuous sound. Well, really we can't perceive such tiny gaps, but a super-powerful alien being might be puzzled as to why we humans listen to such strange "gappy audio"!

Using digital signals

A digital signal is different from its continuous counterpart because, as we've seen, digital signals have gaps between samples. This is illustrated by the dots in Figure 1-1, which are a sampled version of the continuous signal. What happens between the digital signal gaps? The answer is: We simply don't know - the gaps are due to the physical process of sampling. An appreciation of the sampling process provides the key to understanding the discontinuous nature of a digital signal.

Provided the signal is sampled sufficiently rapidly (at the so-called Nyquist frequency), then the gaps become irrelevant to the quality of the user experience of that signal. In other words, a listener to a music track will not perceive the gaps in between the samples, provided the sampling has occurred sufficiently rapidly.

As we'll soon see, continuous and digital signals are close relations to one another. But, it is a one-way relationship, i.e., a digital signal is created from a continuous signal. As noted, it is not possible to create a full-fidelity continuous signal from a digital signal – it will always be an approximation because of the data loss during the sampling and quantization process.

I can still remember the first time I listened to a highly-compressed audio telephone call. It was during a technology exhibition in the UK in the 1990s. The company in question was showcasing its compression products and had a phone at their stand. They invited interested parties to try out a compressed phone conversation. I decided to try and was struck by the slightly tinny and robotic sound of the person at the other end. It was perfectly easy to understand them but the overall experience was a bit machine-like. By stripping out and compressing the human voice, it probably does become more machine-like!

We'll look much more closely at digital signals in the coming chapters.

Chapter 2 Creating a signal with Audacity®

We now look at creating some signals using a popular open source audio management product called Audacity. This will enable you to get a feel for signals in general, including the signals contained in WAV files. As you'll soon see, Audacity can be used as the basis of a kind of signal processing laboratory. So, if you want to use your own machine to follow along with the text, then let's get started by downloading, installing, and running the excellent audio editor, Audacity.

Figure 2-1 illustrates the main Audacity window.

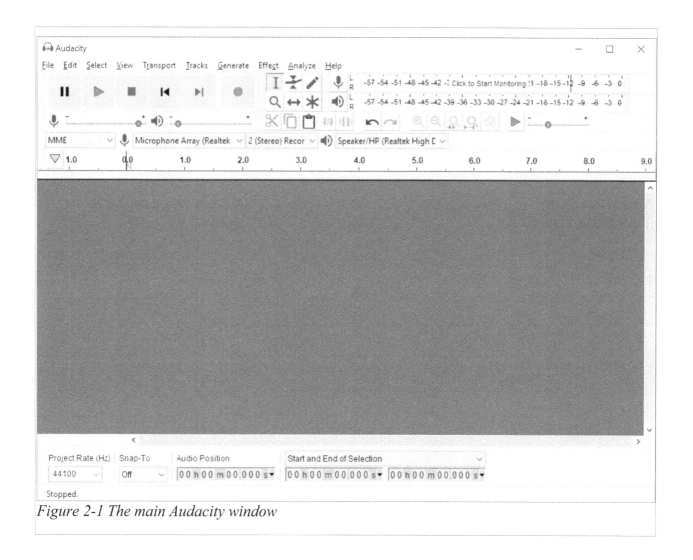

Figure 2-1 The main Audacity window

It's a good idea to play around with the various Audacity menu options just to get a feel for this brilliant application. The help section is comprehensive and has detailed content about audio signals, sampling, aliasing, sample format, compression, and so on.

Let's now create our very first signal for use in Audacity.

Signal Creation with Audacity

Creating a signal in Audacity is as simple as clicking on the Generate menu option and selecting the Tone sub menu as illustrated in Figure 2-2.

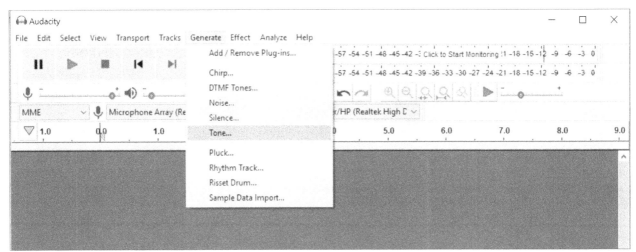

Figure 2-2 Audacity Generate Tone Option

After selecting the Tone option in Figure 2-2, the sub-options for tone generation appear as illustrated in Figure 2-3.

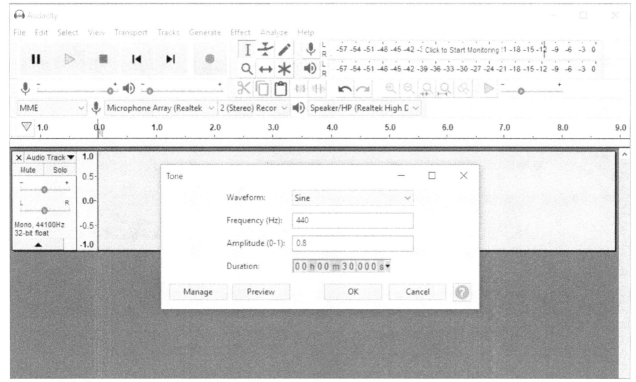

Figure 2-3 Sine wave tone generation

Notice in Figure 2-3, the options to set the following along with their default values:

Waveform type (Sine)Frequency (440)Amplitude (0.8) and Duration (30 seconds)

These parameters give us a lot of control over the generated signal. However, for the moment, let's just keep it simple and accept the default values by clicking OK. The result is a very dense-looking blue signal screen as illustrated in Figure 2-4. Apologies to anyone reading this in black and white, but it hopefully should still be visible as a greyscale image.

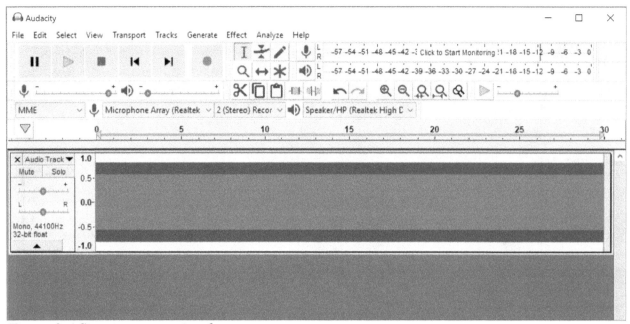

Figure 2-4 Sine wave tone signal

Figure 2-4 is the first signal that we will examine in some detail. It doesn't look terribly interesting.

The signal can be played back by clicking the green play button in the main menu. It sounds pretty awful because it's just a single tone – we're far more used to multi-tone audio, such as, speech and music. Rather than playing back the test signal, it's more interesting to dig into it and examine it a little more closely. So, let's look at the test signal.

So, What Exactly Is Meant by a "Digital" Signal?

To begin with, we can now use our test signal to visually describe exactly what is meant by a digital

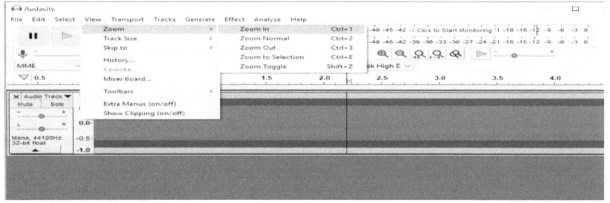

Figure 2-5 View Zoom Menu

signal. Click the View -> Zoom -> Zoom In menu sequence as illustrated in Figure 2-5.

Nothing much seems to happen, right? Well, press the same menu sequence repeatedly, or use the keyboard shortcut (in my case, the shortcut is "Ctrl 1") and watch what happens.

As you repeatedly zoom into the signal, something quite interesting starts to appear – the blue haze starts to disappear and, as illustrated in Figure 2-6, you begin to see the emergence of an underlying sinusoidal wave pattern. Remember, we selected the default sine waveform back in Figure 2-3. So, a sinewave is the expected pattern.

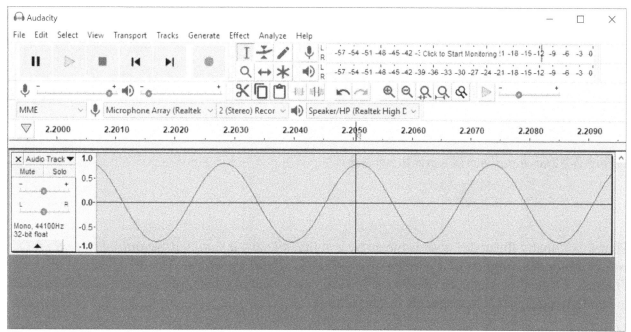

Figure 2-6 The underlying signal begins to appear

There's no real surprise in seeing a sinusoidal pattern in Figure 2-6. This is because, as mentioned above, back in Figure 2-3, we originally generated a sine wave signal. But, compared to the full density signal of Figure 2-5, in Figure 2-6 we can now clearly see the time domain signal shape (or contour) beginning to emerge. The story doesn't stop with the appearance of a sine wave. We can dig even deeper into the signal.

Let's continue to zoom into the signal in Figure 2-6 and you'll notice that the digital nature of the signal starts to appear. In other words, the signal is beginning to separate into its sample components and this is illustrated in Figure 2-7. Remember, the signal is not being changed in any way as we zoom in, we're just changing the perspective and this helps us to look more closely at the constituent elements of the signal. As we'll see later, one of the key parts of DSP is using different perspectives when looking at your signals.

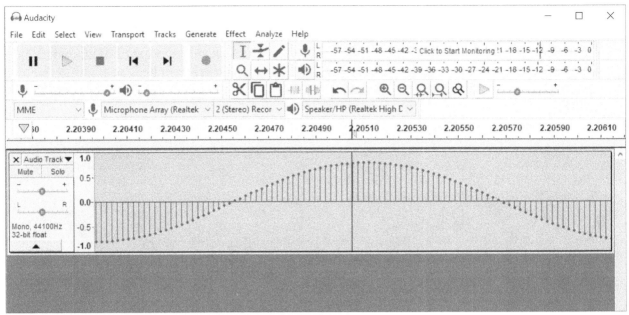

Figure 2-7 The digital world starts to appear

Figure 2-7 finally illustrates what is meant by a digital signal – *a sampled, quantized stream of values along the contours of a previously continuous signal waveform*. The digital signal in Figure 2-7 is just the sequence of dots (or vertical bars), each of which, represents a sample value of the underlying signal at that specific instant in time.

I think it's a good idea to take a long hard look at Figure 2-7 – it represents the very essence of what is called 'digital audio'. In a sense, it shows the way a digital entity, such as, a sampled sine wave, also has an analogue counterpart. A key element in DSP is that the analogue and digital worlds are separate and distinct but they are also inextricably interwoven.

What values do the samples in Figure 2-7 have? Good question. Notice the scale on the left hand side, where the values range from -1.0 to 1.0. All the signal values fall inside this range and each such value represents a sound pressure level for that specific sample of the underlying sound wave.

The Audacity Help menu has some useful details about signal levels and, in particular, what is called clipping. The latter is where a given signal exceeds the allowable range and is clipped or limited so that the excessively large values are modified to sit inside the range.

You can continue to zoom into Figure 2-7 all the way down to just a few samples. It's useful to examine the sample values in this way to get a really solid feel for digital signals in general. You can repeat the complete exercise by generating other signal types, such as, Chirp, DMTF Tones, and so on.

A digital signal is a series of numbers. It really is that simple.

The Sampling ProcessSampling is the mechanism that transforms a continuous signal into a digital signal. A signal is sampled by taking a series of regular snapshots from a continuous signal. After sampling the signal, each value has to be *quantized*, that is, written into a container format. An example container format is a 16-bit integer. Needless to say, this imposes a constraint on the numerical range of the sampled values: some samples may be too large for 16-bits while others may be too small. In both cases, the difference is referred to as the quantization error, which is a kind of noise element.

Our test signal is synthetically generated using Audacity and does not originate as a continuous signal. For this reason, there is no sampling process required. The same is, of course, not true for music or speech that originates in the analogue domain. Such real-world signals have to be converted into digital versions of the original.

DSP

Up to now, we've been examining the test signal in the time domain. While this is interesting and instructive, it's generally not very convenient for either signal analysis or signal processing. Not surprisingly, signal analysis and signal processing are the pillars of DSP and to understand them, we have to look at the frequency domain. Before moving to the frequency domain, let's get a little more hands-on with a test signal.

Generating an audio file

It is possible to save your audio data from within Audacity. The entire project can be saved or you can simply export the audio component using one of the supported file types. Just select File -> Export -> Export as WAV as illustrated in Figure 2-8. Select a suitable file location, provide a file name and then click Save.

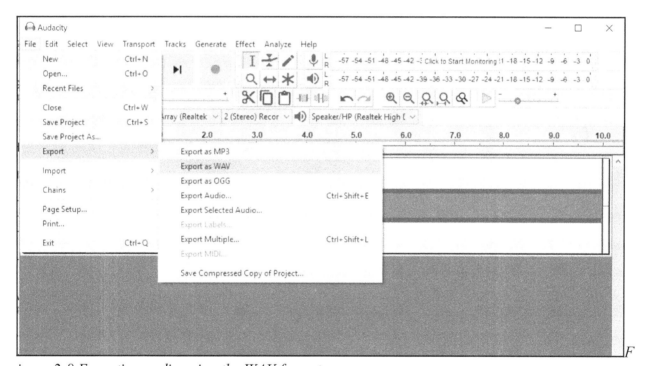

igure 2-8 Exporting audio using the WAV format

At this point, you now have a saved audio file in what can be considered one of the de facto standard audio formats, i.e., WAV. The saved file can be imported back into Audacity (for further processing) or into some other audio editor. The ability to save and reload (and modify) signal data is a key part of the DSP work pipeline.

Signal Frequency

It's useful to get a feel for the term frequency. To take a sinusoidal signal, the frequency is simply the reciprocal of the signal period, i.e., 1/T. The period (T) is one full cycle of the repeating signal; for a sine wave, this is a complete zero-to-zero transition. This can be seen in Figure 2-9 where the signal repeats in a sinusoidal manner. You can also see the zero crossings marked in Figure 2-9.

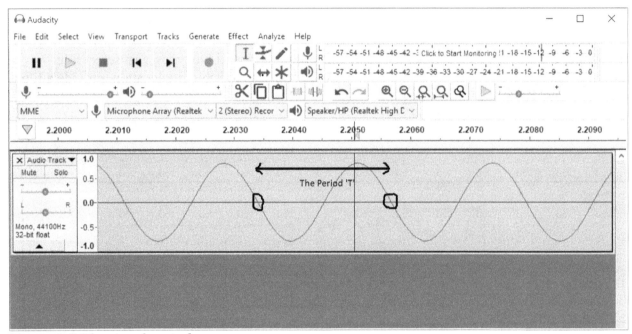

Figure 2-9 The signal period

In Figure 2-9, the period is illustrated as the time gap between three adjacent zero crossings. This is a convenient way to view the period.

Breaking the Monotony

The signals we've ;looked at so far have all been single-tone. This has the merit of allowing us to see the signal envelope as a sinusoidal pattern and we can zoom down much further to see the individual samples. The latter might be considered to be the atoms of the signal.

In the real world, signals tend to multi-tone in nature, such as that illustrated in Figure 2-10.

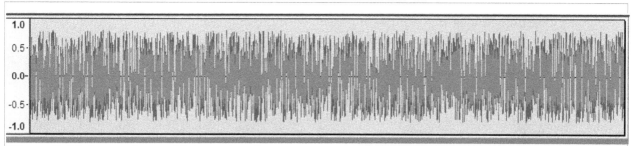
Figure 2-10 A complex multi-tone signal

This signal is more typical of the type of audio wave that is presented to the DSP practitioner. Because the Figure 2-10 signal has a large number of component frequencies, it is more difficult to process than is the case for single-tone signals. To expand on this, what does the spectrum of Figure 2-10 look like? Good question. Here's the frequency spectrum in Figure 2-11.

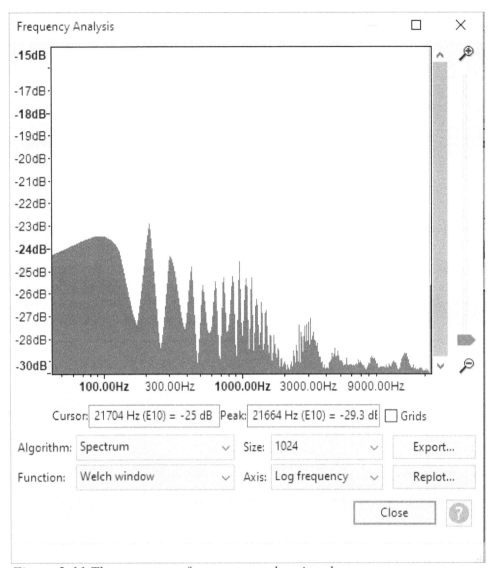

Figure 2-11 The spectrum of a more complex signal

Notice in Figure 2-11 all the peaks and troughs. This models the audio components in the frequency domain. It's important to note that we can convert between the time and frequency domains without any loss of data.

We'll be looking much more closely at this in relation to sampling frequency in the chapters to come.

Chapter 3 Examining Signals In The Frequency Domain

Having viewed the time domain representation of a single-tone test signal and introduced the frequency domain, we can now look at the analysis of such signals using Audacity. This requires us to use the frequency domain. So, let's get stuck in.

Let's refer once again to our single-tone test signal (reproduced below in Figure 3-1).

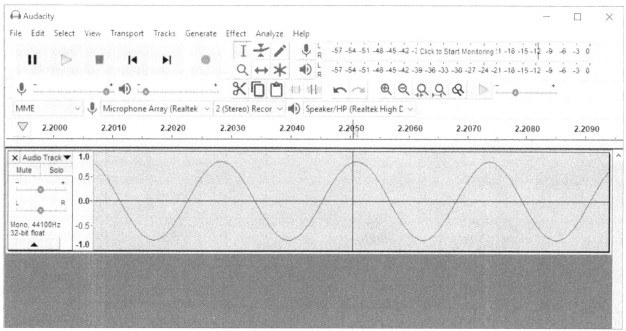

Figure 3-1 Single-tone sinusoidal signal

Recall that the signal in Figure 3-1 is a single-tone, sinusoidal test signal. What does this mean? Well, it means that the signal varies in time in a sinusoidal fashion. In other words, the signal has a rate of change which is governed by a sinusoidal function. Such a signal is quite special because (theoretically) it just repeats endlessly. This means that it has a single frequency component and this can be seen graphically illustrated in Figure 3-2.

Figure 3-2 is the second frequency domain illustration we've seen so far in the book. It's easy to reproduce this in Audacity. Just select the complete signal (e.g., typing Ctrl A) and then click Analyze -> Plot Spectrum. This will then produce the frequency spectrum as illustrated in Figure 3-2.

A spectrum in general can be thought of as a large range of values and this model is also valid for the frequency spectrum. Though, remember that we are looking at different domains in both cases. In the time domain, the rules of engagement are different from those of the frequency domain.

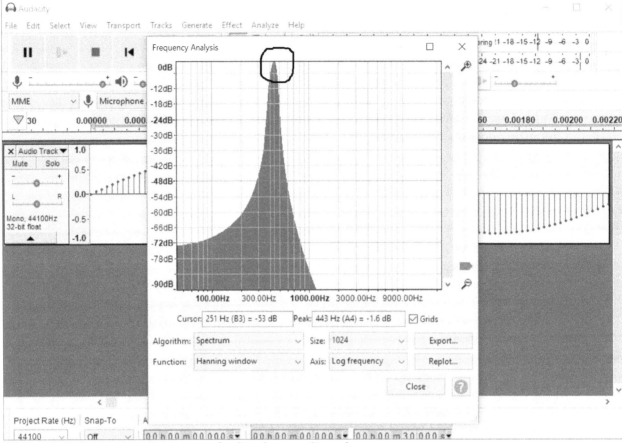

Figure 3-2 Frequency Spectrum of a Single-tone Signal

Notice in Figure 3-2, the marked peak value in the spectrum. This peak value represents the principal sinusoidal frequency component from the original test signal. In short, this peak represents the single tone that is present in our test signal.

In Figure 3-2, we're looking at the frequency spectrum of the signal. This is just as valid as the time domain representation from Figure 3-1. But, as we'll see later, looking at signals in the frequency domain is an extremely powerful technique for both signal analysis and signal processing.

Before we dig deeper still into DSP, let's have a small digression to assist you (assuming, of course, you need any assistance) with getting up to speed with Audacity and signals in general.

Dog Whistles and Human Hearing

Let's generate a new sinusoidal signal, just like we did way back in Figure 2-3, except this time pick a much larger frequency. Start with 5000Hz and then play back the generated signal. ***Please be sure to keep the volume low on your speakers – single-tone signals don't make for particularly pleasant listening.*** Then, create a new signal using 6000Hz and play it back. Repeat the procedure a few times.

As you increase the frequency, you'll reach a point where you can no longer hear the playback. This is simply an illustration of the threshold of normal human hearing. Depending on age, the range of human hearing typically peaks around the 9000Hz mark. Though, young people can theoretically hear all the way up to 20,000Hz.

Dog whistles emit sound in what is called the ultrasonic frequency range, which starts around 20,000Hz and increases up to several gigahertz. The sound signals are exactly the same as human-audible sound, it's just that humans can't hear them. This example illustrates the relatively narrow range of audio which is human-audible versus the range that our canine friends can hear.

A Feline-Unfriendly Hoover

The current model of domestic hoover we use in our house is a popular brand. We've had it for a few years and it sounds pretty loud to me, almost to the point of being uncomfortable. The two cats concur and both of them generally prefer to go out even in the rain when the hoover is in use.

I got a little curious about this and took a sample recording of the hoover. I imported the audio signal into Audacity and the spectrum showed a really big peak around 11,000Hz. I'm not sure if the cats couldn't bear this 11kHz component, but it was seemingly painful to humans and cats alike.

Once the fearful machine was switched off, the two cats would appear soon after on a window sill and cautiously return to their inner sanctum.

Frequency Spectrum

Having now viewed a graph showing the frequency spectrum of the test signal, let's have a look at the actual numbers in the graph. Listing 1 illustrates an excerpt from the frequency spectrum for the test signal in Figure 3-2. Don't worry about the minus sign in front of the numbers. It's a logarithmic ratio. We'll explain this later. For the moment, just think of the numbers in the Level column as: *smaller is larger*.

Frequency (Hz)	Level (dB)
43.066406	-151.350510
86.132813	-151.911957
129.199219	-152.082260
172.265625	-151.681885
215.332031	-151.940521
258.398438	-151.884537
301.464844	-151.654846
344.531250	-151.371521
387.597656	-152.154266
430.664063	-151.537033
473.730469	-151.824509
516.796875	-151.483017
559.863281	-151.786316
602.929688	-151.276367
645.996094	-151.841980
689.062500	-151.464584

Listing 1 Frequency spectrum values

The values on the left hand side of Listing 1 are frequency and on the right, we have the actual amplitude values in the frequency spectrum. The values of -151dB are in fact very low, essentially zero in the time domain. So, where is our expected peak value – the one that represents the sinusoidal test tone that we saw in Figure 3-2?

Looking down the numbers (at frequencies higher than those in Listing 1), we get a section like Listing 2. Notice the increase in the Level column values as compared to Listing 1. The peak value is marked in bold italics in Listing 2 and has the value: -1.940448.

Frequency (Hz)	Level (dB)	
8828.613281	-69.633736	
8871.679688	-61.976044	
8914.746094	-50.167332	
8957.812500	-7.684387	
9000.878906	*-1.940448*	----->>> *Peak Spectrum Value*
9043.945313	-8.214970	
9087.011719	-52.484642	
9130.078125	-64.870430	
9173.144531	-73.276741	
9216.210938	-79.798645	
9259.277344	-85.205345	
9302.343750	-89.877907	
9345.410156	-94.041397	
9388.476563	-97.831825	

Listing 2 Frequency spectrum values containing the peak

This is our peak value, which represents the underlying frequency selected at the time of signal generation. Notice the way we viewed the signal spectrum data by inspection? While this is often not feasible on account of the sheer quantity of data involved, in some cases, it is possible and is often useful. Where the data is too large for manual inspection, there are other techniques that can be used for visualization, such as, software graphing.

A Multi-tone Signal

It's a simple matter in Audacity to create a two-tone signal. Just create one signal of say 10 seconds duration with a frequency of 5000Hz. Then, move to the end of the first signal by clicking the Skip to end button on the top menu. At the end of the first signal component, create a second adjacent component with a frequency of 15000Hz also with a duration of 10 seconds. In total, the two-tone signal is then 20 seconds in duration. Plotting the spectrum of such a signal then looks like that illustrated in Figure 3-3.

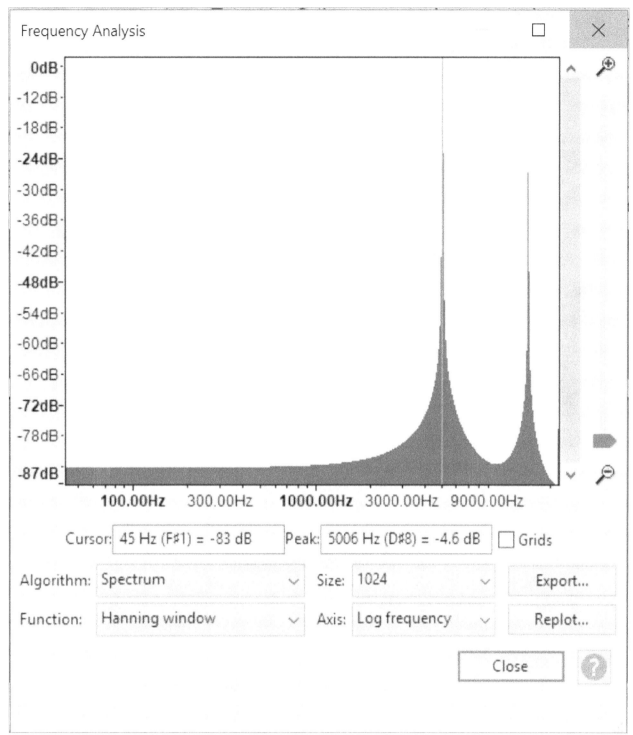

Figure 3-3 A multi-tone audio test signal

Notice the two peaks in Figure 3-3 – one for each of the constituent frequencies. Normal audio, such as speech or music, has a wide range of constituent frequencies. In contrast with the test signals we've looked at so far, normal audio is rich in content and complex in structure. Let's now look a little more closely at the signal content, i.e., the constituent samples. To do this, close the frequency analysis window and click the Audio Position dropdown control as illustrated in Figure 3-4.

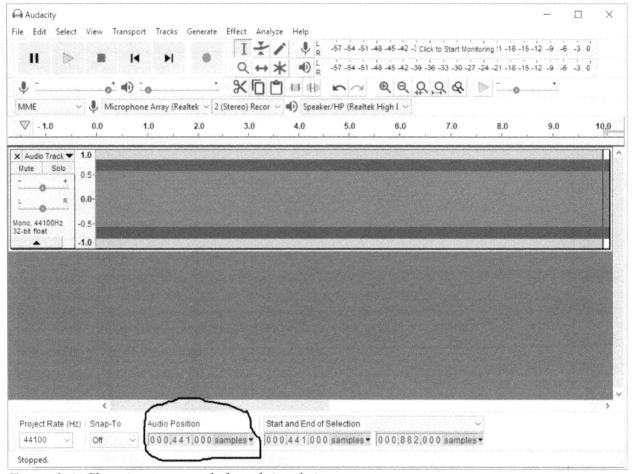

Figure 3-4: Changing to a sample-based signal view

Select the 'Samples' option and you'll see the signal representation change from the default time-based view to the sample-based view. Then, zoom in just like we did earlier and you'll see the two tones in the signal as illustrated in Figure 3-5.

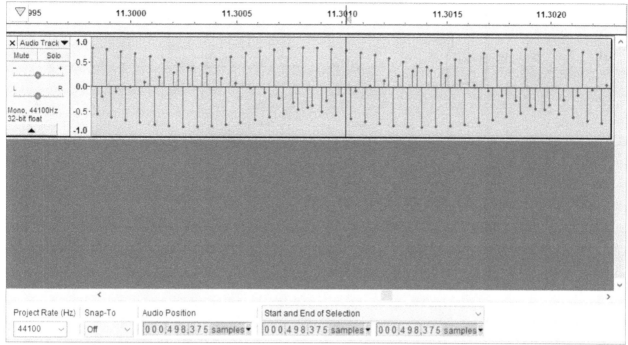

Figure 3-5: The two tones in the test signal viewed as samples

Notice in Figure 3-5, I've selected one of the samples in the signal (see the vertical black bar in the middle of Figure 3-5). What effect does clicking have? Well, look at the value in the 'Audio Position' at the bottom of Figure 3-5 – it's now set to the value 498,375, which is the offset (or position) of the associated individual sample in the overall signal. This illustrates the way that signals can get very large very quickly. It also shows that digital signals are basically just a collection of numbers.

Another key element in Figures 3-4 and 3-5 is the 'Project Rate (Hz)' setting, which is visible in the bottom left corner and has the value 44,100. This is in fact the sampling frequency and is perhaps the most important element in the signal. What does the sampling frequency mean? Well, it means that the signal in question has 44,100 samples in each second of duration – this is quite a lot of data! If you click the 'Skip to End' button on the top-level menu as illustrated at the top of Figure 3-6, this will move the window to the very end of the signal.

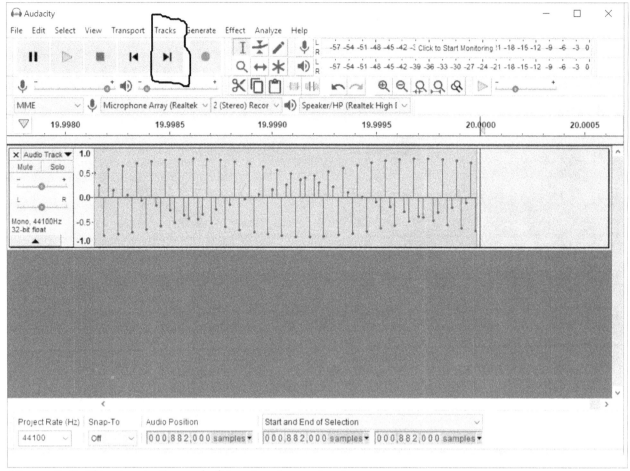

Figure 3-6: Skipping to the end of the signal sample view

How do we know we're at the end of the signal? Well, look at the audio position at the bottom of Figure 3-6, which now has a value of 882,000 samples. Our signal is 20 seconds long and each second has a total of 44,100 samples (i.e., remember the sample rate is 44,100 samples per second). So, 20-seconds worth of signal has 20 * 44,100 samples or 882,000 samples which is in fact the value in the Audio Position illustrated in Figure 3-6. Another indicator that we're at the end of the signal is the lack of any values in the right hand side of the signal depiction. It's useful to be able to 'move' around a signal in this way.

This discussion illustrates one of the most noticeable aspects of signals and DSP in general: Signals have a lot of data in them. A few minutes of audio can consume a lot of disk space. Processing this level of data presents a lot of challenges to the DSP practitioner. This is one of the reasons why DSP algorithms have traditionally been realised in hardware rather than software. However, the widespread availability of computing power has done much to change the balance of hardware versus software.

In the next chapter, we'll look at how to change a signal by using the technique of filtering. This is one of the cornerstone techniques of DSP.

Chapter 4 Filtering Signals

So far, we've seen mostly simple, single-tone signals. It's interesting and useful to examine such signals in the time domain where they manifest as a range of numbers changing in a sinusoidal manner. We've also seen that the signal can be converted from the time domain into the frequency domain. This has numerous advantages for the DSP practitioner. Firstly, the tone content in the signal becomes clear in the form of one or more peaks in the frequency spectrum.

I note in passing that moving from the time domain into the frequency domain is not one-way. It is perfectly possible to move back to the time domain. In fact, if an audio signal is modified in the frequency domain, then that effect can then be observed by listening to the signal in the time domain. Clearly, to do the latter we must transform the signal from the frequency domain back into the time domain.

While it's interesting and instructive to look at the signal structure in the time domain, what if we want to modify the signal? For this, we can use filtering. Using one of our test signals, let's now see what signal filtering is about.

Figure 4-1 illustrates the frequency spectrum of a multi-tone signal. Notice the two peaks in the spectrum. These peaks correspond with the two frequencies I selected during signal generation: 5000Hz and 15000Hz, respectively. But, you can of course use any frequencies you like in your own generated test signal.

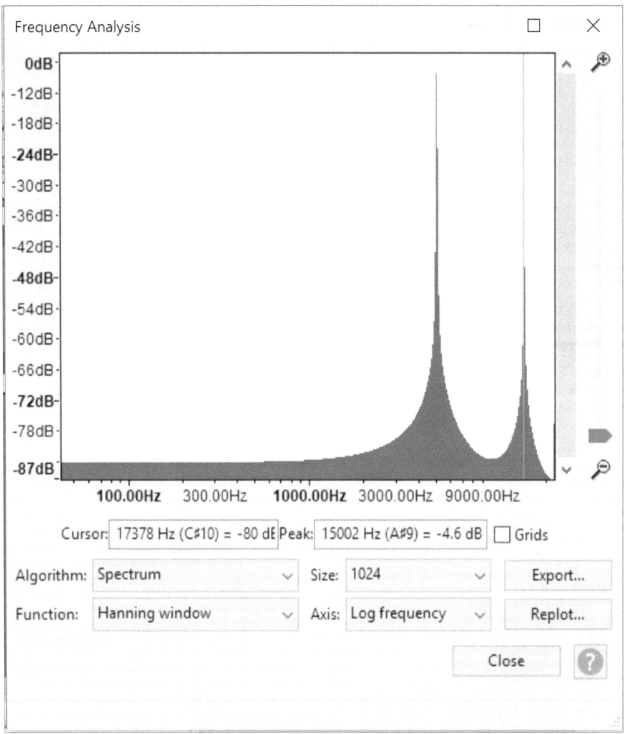

Figure 4-1: A two-tone audio test signal spectrum

Let's say we decided, as DSP practitioners, to remove or filter out the upper frequency element, i.e., the 15000Hz component. So, we want to see just one peak in the spectrum. This can be achieved using the filtering option in Audacity to produce the modified spectrum illustrated in Figure 4-2.

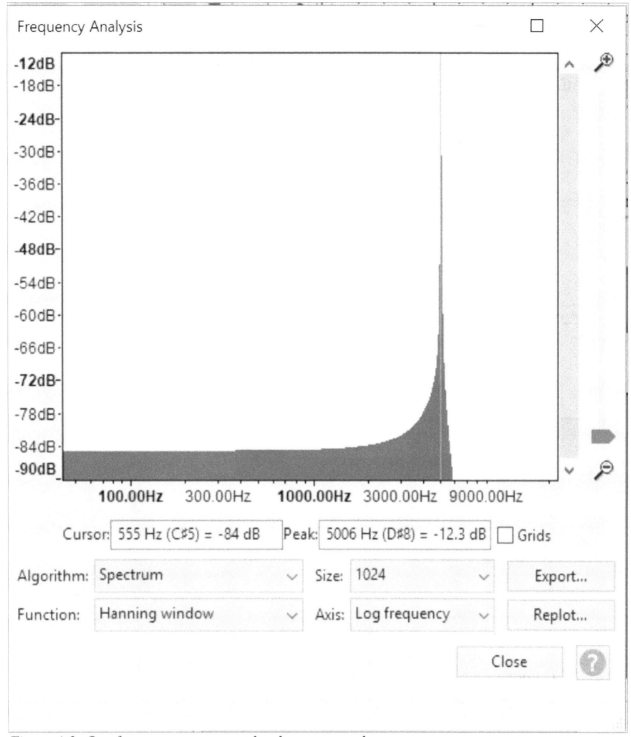

Figure 4-2: One frequency component has been removed

Figure 4-2 illustrates the power of DSP filtering. The signal has been modified in accordance with our wishes and we are left with just a single frequency. We can, if required, now reconstruct the signal with the modified spectrum. This is a key point to note and is well worth repeating:

It is possible to go from the time domain to the frequency domain and vice versa with no loss of data.

In the case of our Audacity test signal, there is no required transformation back to the time domain. This is because the spectrum analysis is done from the time domain, which means that the spectral components are overlaid on the time domain signal. So, to go back to the time domain, it is of course sufficient to simply close the spectrum window as illustrated in Figure 4-3.

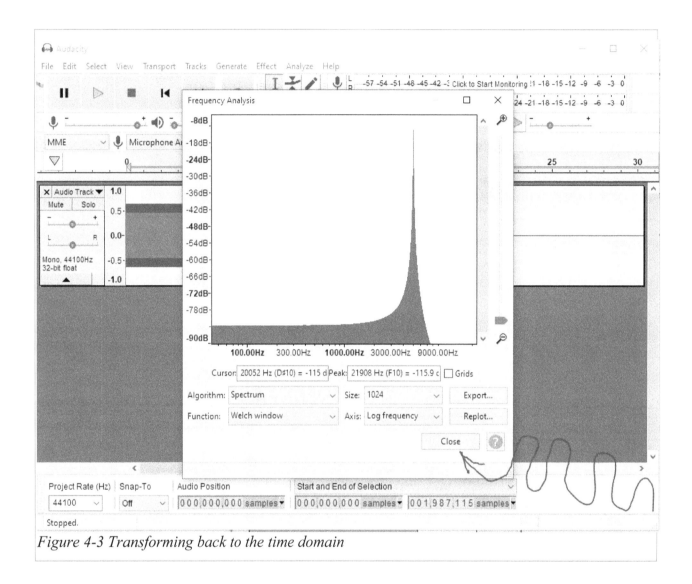

Figure 4-3 Transforming back to the time domain

In practice, transformation to and from the frequency domain will usually involve the use of tools such as DFT software.

Chapter 5 The DSP Process

An important part of any technical work procedure is the process used and DSP is no different in this regard. For this reason, a description is now provided for a basic DSP process. This is simply the typically iterative procedure used to acquire, analyze, modify, and view signals as they move through the work pipeline.

As with any development process, the workflow may be driven by tickets or 'issues'. This is simply where a given piece of development work is recorded as a text description and assigned a ticket number. The ticket can then be assigned to an individual or team for estimation, design, and implementation. If this sounds a little like a help desk workflow, that's because it's actually quite similar. The important point is that the work is recorded as it progresses through the organizational workflow. There are numerous tools for managing this type of workflow-based development.

There are no hard and fast rules for defining a process for DSP development, but the following is one approach that can be applied to audio work:

1. Signal Import
2. Review/Listen
3. Analyze
4. Modify
5. Review/Listen
6. Save and Signal Export

As the process is iterative in nature, it is entirely likely that the above steps will be executed numerous times over the course of a project.

Let's now look at the process details.

Signal Import

During signal import, you typically acquire the incoming signal. The signal may be provided to you by someone else or you may acquire it autonomously,e.g., using some sort of recording facility. In any case, the signal import phase typically introduces the signal into your 'laboratory'. The latter may be some software tool, such as, Audacity. Or it may be a specialized workbench created specifically for your project.

One interesting source of audio is that from Web radio stations. This is a great example of mixing old and new technology. Many if not all radio stations now stream their content onto the web. Software tools can be used to capture such audio, e.g., for listening to station content at a later time or for carrying out DSP work on the content.

Review/Listen

Once the analysis signal has been imported, it is then ready to be reviewed. This might be as simple as listening to the underlying audio or this step might encompass visually reviewing the contours of the signal. It is also possible to use some software-based graphing tool to view the signal components. The review/listen phase of the pipeline is extremely important and may be revisited multiple times in order to verify signal integrity.

In any case, this leads us into the beginning of the signal analysis phase.

Analyze

During the analysis phase, the signal is examined in more detail. Typically, this involves conversion of the signal from the time domain into the frequency domain. Once the latter occurs, it is no longer useful or feasible to listen to the "audio" because we are no longer in the time domain. For this reason, the analysis is often more visual or computational in nature. We can see an example of visual analysis of a converted signal in Figure 5-1 which illustrates two spectral peaks.

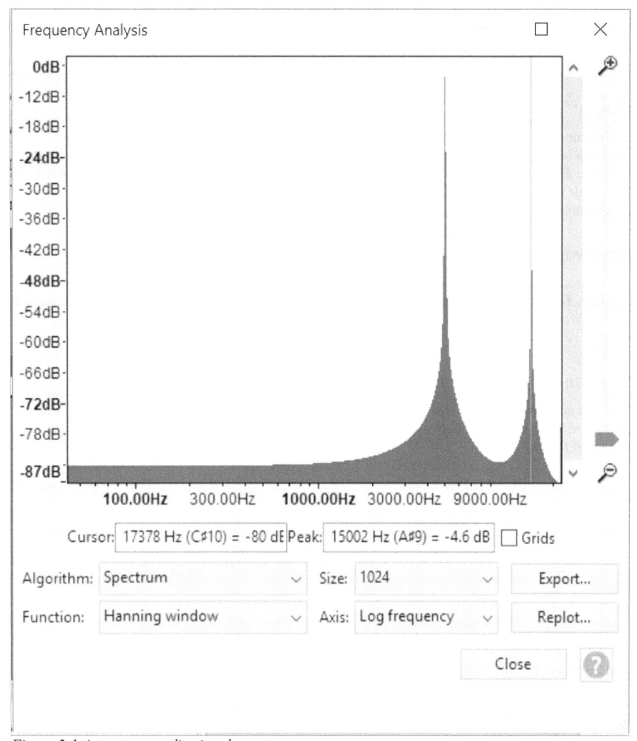

Figure 5-1 A two-tone audio signal spectrum

Figure 5-1 provides a useful check on the frequency content of the signal. This is important for those cases where your work involves modification of the spectrum, such as, filtering out a given frequency range. It is entirely possible that, due to a bug in your code, you may inadvertently change a two-tone signal into a no-tone signal!

In addition to a visual check, specialized software tools, e,g., tools you write yourself or open source tools, or commercial tools, can be used to extract even more information from the spectrum. We'll see examples of such tools in later chapters.

The analysis phase itself is also often iterative in nature (for example, changing the settings in Figure 5-1, such as the algorithm, function, etc.) and may be revisited many times over before moving to the next phase. The important point to note is that the overall process is typically flexible in nature.

Modify

During modification, you change the underlying signal, e.g., filtering out some component or changing some values. We've already seen an example of filtering out a single tone. Noise reduction is a more complex version of this type of DSP procedure. Signal modification is not without risk! It is possible to inadvertently destroy a signal, for example, by changing or removing some component. The other steps in the DSP process can and should help to avoid such issues.

Review/Listen

After modification, we need to check the signal is intact and has been changed in the manner required. This is an important step because it allows for error checking, just in case the modification is not correct. An algorithm that incorrectly changes a signal might render it meaningless to a listener. For this reason, we revisit our step 2 and repeat the review/listen procedure as appropriate.

Save and Signal Export

Once we are happy with the DSP phase, the signal can be saved to disk and then exported to the next stage in the pipeline. Tools such as Audacity provide facilities to save audio to disk using a variety of formats.

Chapter 6 DSP and the Discrete Fourier Transform (DFT)

Having arrived at a simple process for DSP work, we come now to the issue of analytical tools for looking more deeply at signals. Signals tend to be very data-rich with lots and lots of associated data points. Indeed, just looking at a time domain signal often provides little or no information on the underlying spectral characteristics. Fortunately, there is a tool which can help to transform the time domain signal into a frequency-based counterpart. This tool is called the DFT. There are of course other tools, but the DFT is an excellent starting point.

There are several approaches to using the DFT. Audacity has its own inbuilt DFT facilities. You can also download one of the many freely-available DFT tools. In this chapter, we'll look at using the Audacity DFT tools. In fact, you've already seen the Audacity-integrated DFT tools in action in the previous chapters.

To get started, let's go back to the two-tone test signal we used in Chapters 4 and 5. The spectrum for this signal is illustrated in Figure 6-1.

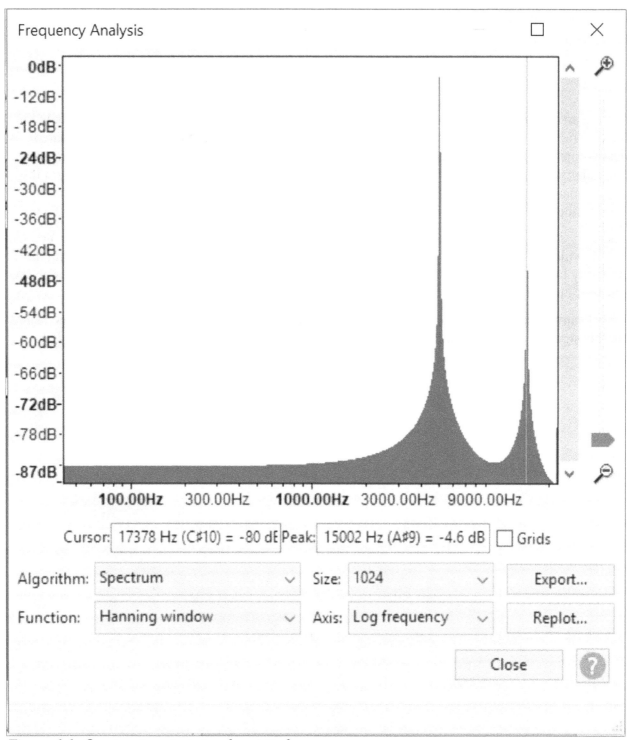

Figure 6-1: Our two-tone test signal revisited

Let's look a little more closely at Figure 6-1. Notice the familiar two 'humps' on the right hand side of Figure 6-1 – one for each of the two constituent frequency tones.

The graph in Figure 6-1 is in fact derived from a DFT algorithm provided as part of Audacity itself. The Audacity tools allow you to generate the spectrum for any type of multi-tone signal.

Spectral Analysis Using the DFT

For example, Figure 6-2 illustrates the spectrum of a signal generated using the Audacity 'noise' template. To generate such a signal, simply click the Audacity Generate menu option (from way back in Figure 2-1) followed by selecting the submenu item Noise.

To then generate the spectrum in Figure 6-2, just select the menu item Audacity Analyze and finally click the Plot Spectrum... submenu item.

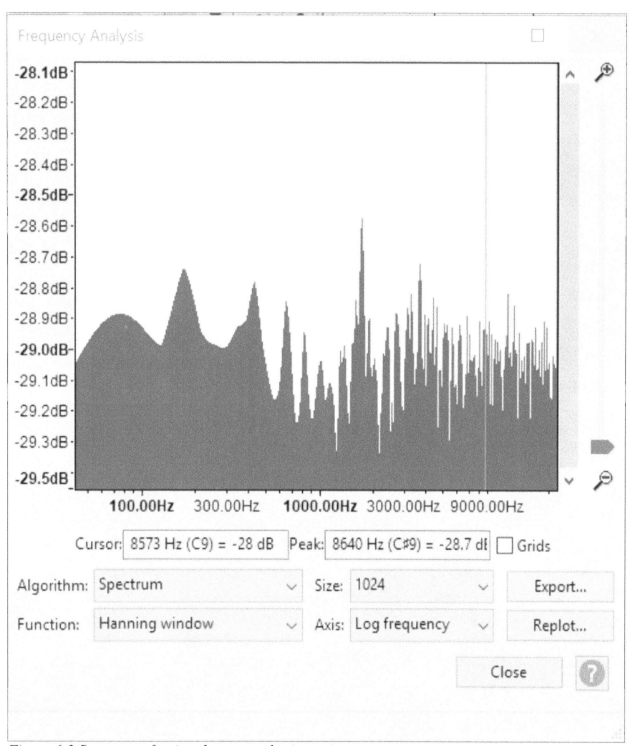

Figure 6-2 Spectrum of a signal generated using noise

Notice the spectral richness of Figure 6-2 as compared to the relative simplicity of the spectra of Figure 6-1 and our earlier test signals. Figure 6-2 contains many peaks and troughs. In practice, the signals of interest in DSP work tend to be complex and rich in content. It is possible to change the visualization in Figure 6-2 by adjusting some key settings.

In Figure 6-3, we can see some important marked elements (at the bottom of the diagram) that are used to interact with and modify the spectrum contents.

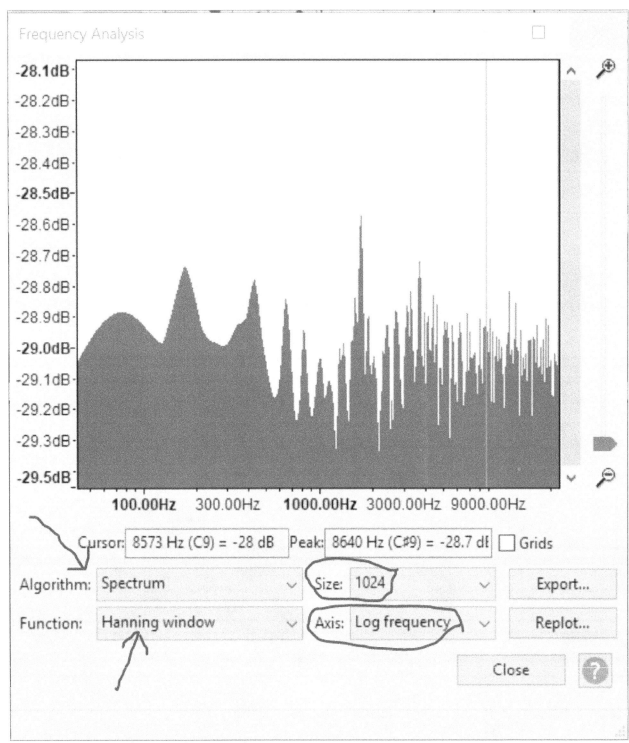

Figure 6-3 Spectral manipulation tools

In Figure 6-3, the Algorithm we use is the default setting called 'Spectrum'. As noted earlier, the detail in the upper half of Figure 6-3 is produced using the inbuilt DFT tools in Audacity.

The Function or window method is also illustrated in Figure 6-3. We use the default Hanning window and this is described in the next section.

The Size setting is the number of signal samples used for the spectrum analysis. Again, we use the default value of 1024 (typically, this is some power of 2). The number of signal samples is often referred to as 'N' in the DSP literature. We return to this key parameter a little later.

The final setting of interest in Figure 6-3 is the 'Axis'. This parameter indicates that the vertical axis is expressed in logarithmic terms. The use of a logarithmic scale helps in viewing the data by reducing the value range to a more manageable scale. It also makes it easier to distinguish between spectral values that are numerically close to each other but functionally different.

DFT Windowing

Window functions are really important in DSP. This is because we are often interested in just a section of a signal. Or the signal itself may be relatively short in duration. So, rather than just applying a DFT to the signal, an important first step is passing the signal data through a window function. So, what does this windowing achieve? Well, one thing windowing does is to minimise or (ideally) avoid the introduction of false spectral content.

The false spectral content is related to the points of signal truncation, i.e., the start and end of the signal. A windowing function, such as, Hanning, has the beneficial effect of smoothing out such sudden signal discontinuities.

The selected window function multiplies each signal sample with the result that there is a gradual tapering off of the signal at the beginning and end.

So, that's a brief description of the theory. How does it work out in practice when you change these key parameters? To answer this, let's return to our single-tone test signal as illustrated in Figure 6-4. For this signal, I've selected the Hamming window function.

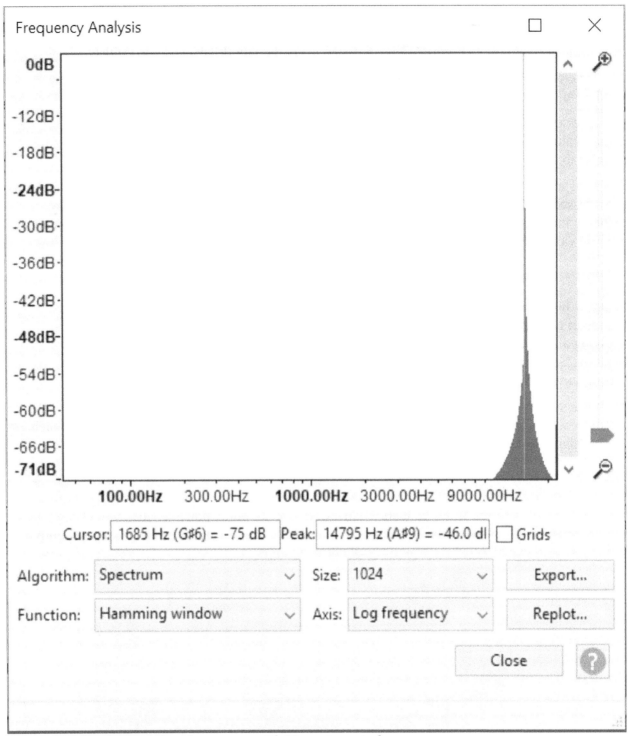

Figure 6-4 Single-tone signal spectrum with Hamming window

Nothing too dramatic from what we've seen earlier. Now, for comparison, I'll select the Hanning window option and this gives us Figure 6-5.

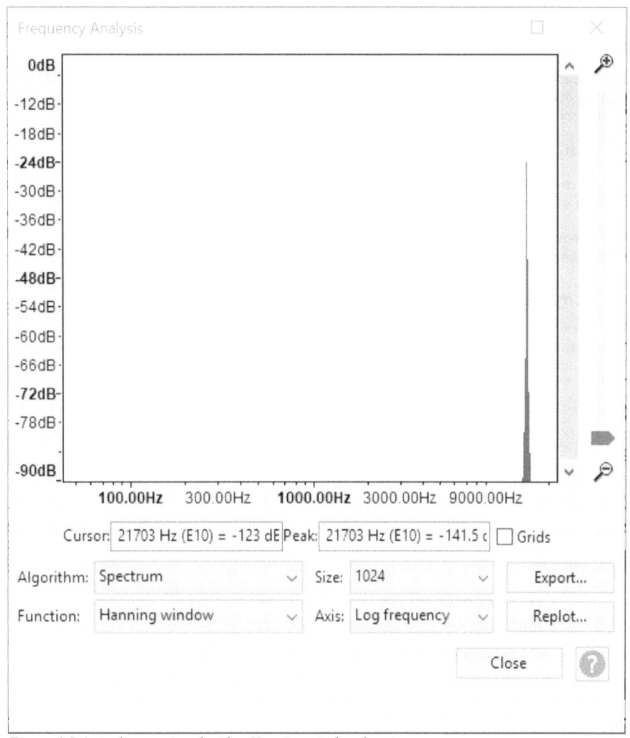

Figure 6-5 A single-tone signal with a Hanning window function

Figures 6-4 and 6-5 look very similar and they are similar. But, there is one key and powerful difference. Look at the width of the spectral peak in both diagrams. In the Figure 6-5 Hanning window case, the peak is much more narrowly defined. This can be very beneficial during the signal analysis phase, for example, narrowly defined peaks can make it easier to extract key signal features – a case of 'less is more'.

The wider peak in Figure 6-4 essentially leaks into the adjacent frequencies and this introduces undesirable content. In effect, in spectra such as those in Figure 6-4 and Figure 6-5, we may see false content or artifacts being introduced into the adjacent analysis frequencies. Compensating for such unwanted artifacts is an important element of DSP algorithms and may require repeatedly applying an algorithm.

This discussion is a good illustration of the need for an iterative DSP process as discussed earlier. Iterating over the same spectral data using different tools and/or tool options helps in arriving at a satisfactory conclusion.

The moral of the story is:

For effective DSP, use all available tools and techniques to solve your specific problem and don't forget to use a good DSP process.

Before moving on, it is worth mentioning that Audacity has another important benefit for students of DSP: Open source code. This is described in the following section.

Audacity Note

One important aspect of Audacity to bear in mind is that it is free and open source. So, you are able to look into and modify the source code itself. This further emphasises the importance of Audacity as a tool for learning DSP.

DFT Analysis Frequencies

The following describes the notion of DFT analysis frequencies. One of the surprising insights provides by DSP is the fact that all signals can be decomposed into a series of sine waves or frequencies. It is this central pillar of DSP that can cause a lot of confusion. Richard Lyons goes into a great deal of detail exploring this topic in his excellent book: " Understanding Digital Signal Processing" [1].

The key thing to understand is that when you derive the DFT for a given signal, there are three key elements:

1. Sampling frequency
2. The number of signal points
3. The number of DFT bins

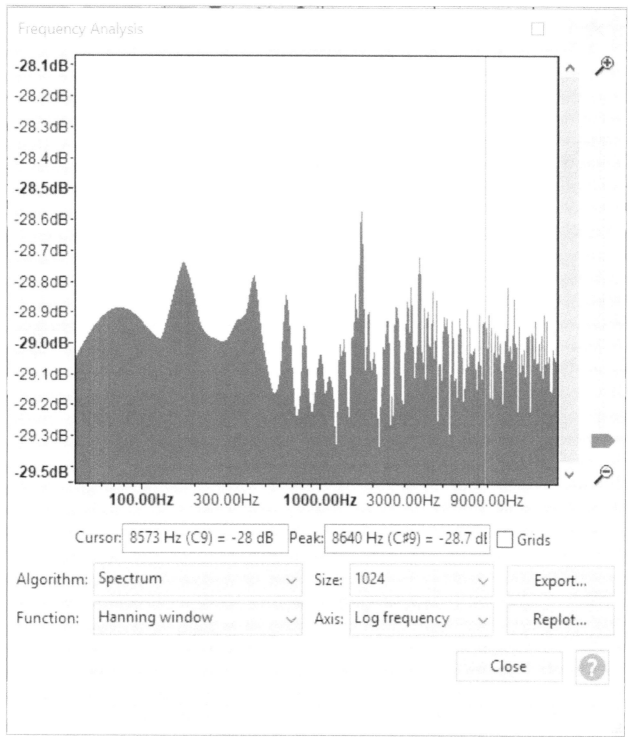

Figure 6-6 The DFT analysis frequencies

Let's expand on this a little by looking back at one of the earlier signals as illustrated in Figure 6-6.

Looking at Figure 6-6, where do we find the sampling frequency and the number of signal points? To answer the first question, we have to go back to the time domain signal (as illustrated in Figure 6-7) to see the sampling frequency. Before we do that, we can extract the number of signal points from Figure 6-6. Can you see it? Well, it has the value 1024 as indicated by the Size field.

Now, let's get the sampling frequency from Figure 6-7.

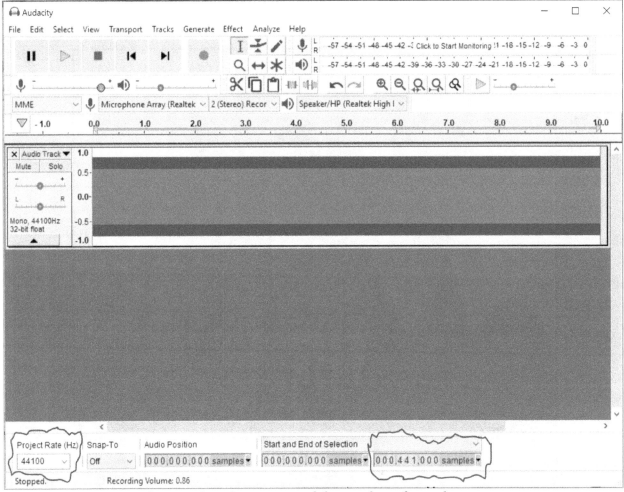

Figure 6-7 Extracting the sampling frequency and the number of samples

Notice in Figure 6-7, I've highlighted the project rate on the bottom left (this is actually the sampling frequency) and on the bottom right, you can see the number of samples (441,000).

In passing, let's figure out how to calculate the latter value. To do this, you need to know the duration of the signal. During signal generation, I used a value of 10 seconds for the signal duration as illustrated in Figure 6-8. In Figure 6-7, you can also see the signal duration is 10 seconds.

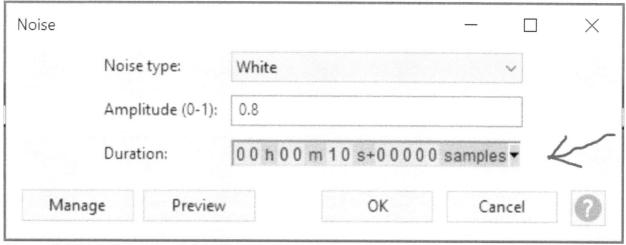

Figure 6-8 Setting the signal duration

So, putting Figures 6-7 and 6-8 together, the sampling frequency is 44,100 and the signal duration is 10 seconds. So, we have 44,100 samples for each second of audio. We have 10 seconds of audio, which therefore gives us a total number of samples of 441,000.

While the above calculation seems rather obvious, it is a useful exercise. It helps in gaining perspective on signals by being able to move between sampling frequencies, signal duration, and the number of samples in a given signal. Such calculations can form an important part of the DSP process as discussed earlier.

We can now dig into the notion of DFT analysis frequencies. This is a direct analogue (in the frequency domain this time) of the time domain sample values that we saw way back in Figure 2-7.

The Analysis Frequencies

Figures 6-7 and 6-8 provide us with a sampling frequency is 44,100 and a total number of samples of 441,000. In Figure 6-6, the number of samples used in the spectrum analysis has the value 1024. So, it's a small part of the overall number of samples (of 441,000).

The formula used to derive the analysis frequencies is:

$$\textit{Analysis Frequency(m) = m* Sampling Frequency / N}$$

The value m refers to the DFT slot or bin. The sampling frequency is 44,100 and the value of N is 1024. So, our signal in the frequency domain contains analysis frequencies as produced by the above formula.

For a value of m = 0, we have 0Hz.

For a value of m = 1, we have 44,100 / 1024 or 43.07Hz.

For a value of m = 2, we have 44,100 / 1024 or 86.13Hz.

These values are the component frequencies of our signal. One might consider them to be the 'atoms' that go together to make up the signal in the frequency domain. Let's have a look at Figure

6-9 to see a visual depiction of the idea of analysis frequencies.

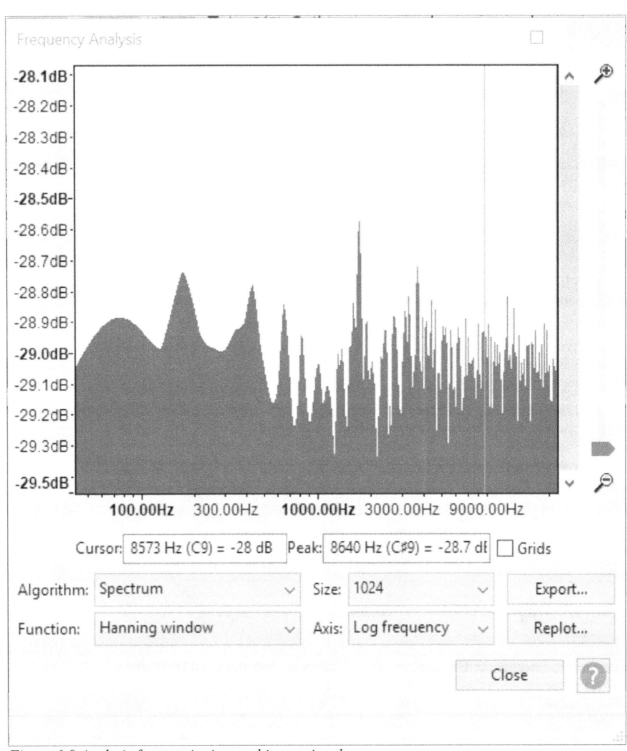

Figure 6-9 Analysis frequencies in a multi-tone signal

The combination of all of the values on the horizontal axis in Figure 6-9 describes the full range of analysis frequencies in the signal.

This is part of the magic of the DFT and is analogous to the way in which we delved into the audio signal way back in Figure 2-7. While the DFT data and the signal data (from Figure 2-7) are from different domains (frequency versus time), both representations illustrate the manner in which we can usefully break down the data.

Let's now look a little more at the important issue of spectral leakage.

Spectral Leakage

When a signal contains more than one component frequency, we start to see the effects of spectral leakage. What does this look like? In Figure 6-10, we have the spectrum of a two-tone signal. The only major difference between this spectrum and the ones we looked at earlier is the choice of window function. In Figure 6-10 we use the Bartlett window.

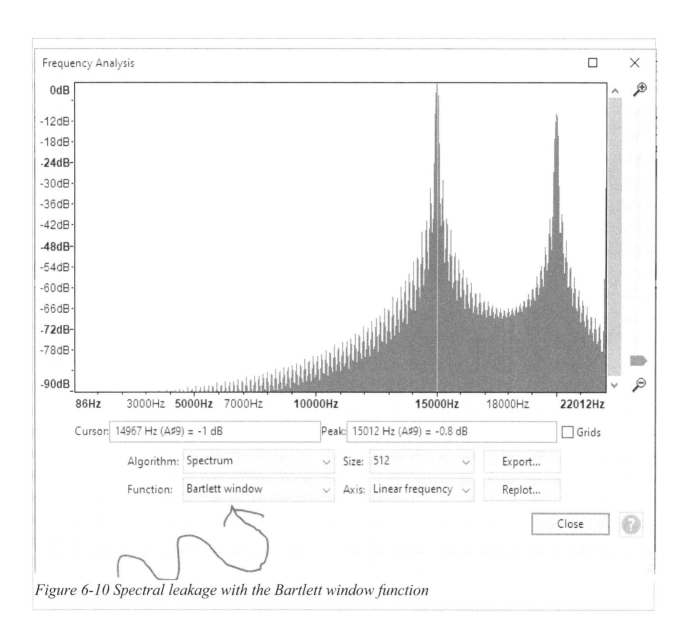

Figure 6-10 Spectral leakage with the Bartlett window function

Notice the many additional peaks and troughs in Figure 6-10. That's a lot of extra spectral content above and beyond our known two tones. This is spectral leakage. Let's look at the same signal with a different window function. In Figure 6-11, we use the Rectangular window function.

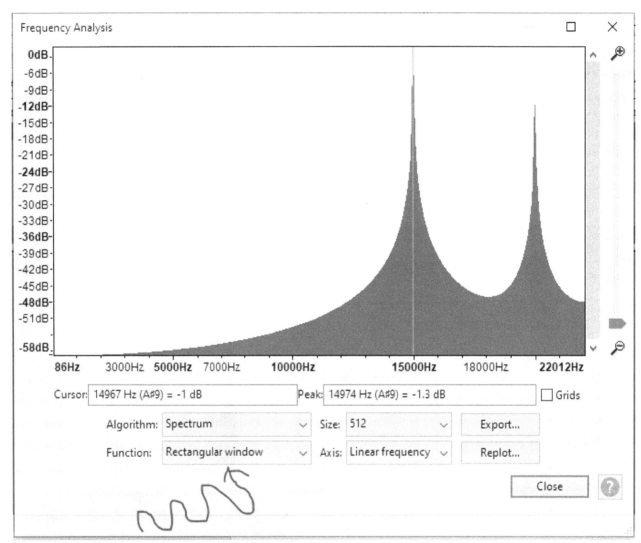

Figure 6-11 Spectral leakage with the rectangular window function

Notice in Figure 6-11, the way the two peaks are wider and they merge into each other. This is leakage caused by the discontinuities at either end of the rectangular window function. The rectangular window function is somewhat special because it provides no tapering off of the signal. This means that the sudden change at the edges of the window function causes spectral leakage.

Using yet another window function (the Hanning window function) in Figure 6-12, we see much less spectral spread.

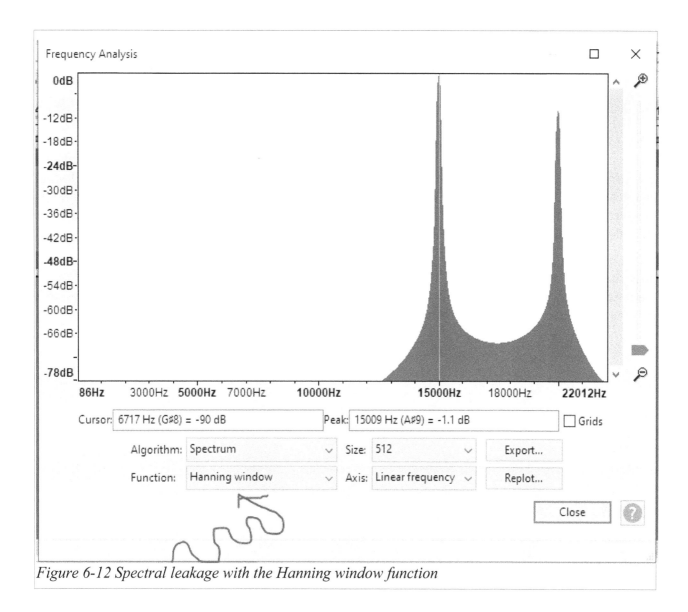

Figure 6-12 Spectral leakage with the Hanning window function

From these different illustrations, we can see that the choice of window function can have important consequences for the resolution of the peaks and troughs in your signal spectra. Again, we see the merit of an iterative and experimental DSP process.

For more information on spectral leakage, a good reference is:
https://en.wikipedia.org/wiki/Spectral_leakage.

In short, getting to grips with DSP involves a lot of shifts of perspective. We'll look at another tool that helps facilitate a different perspective in the next chapter. This tool is called GNU Octave.

Chapter 7 Adding GNU Octave to the DSP Work Toolkit

GNU Octave [2] is another really useful tool for perspective changing in DSP work. Broadly used for the same purpose as the commercial product MATLAB, Octave is available on most modern platforms and comes in the form of either a command line utility or a graphical environment. In this chapter, we'll have an introductory look at Octave. I won't go too much into the details of installing Octave; there's lots of content on YouTube that explains how to do the setup and generally get started with Octave.

For Windows users, the installed setup looks like that illustrated in Figure 7-1a. This is arrived at after running a downloadable installer. In passing, make sure to check that the signature value on the download location matches that signature calculated from the downloaded file. This is to verify that the download hasn't been tampered with.

GnuOctave > octave-6.4.0-w64

Name	Date modified	Type	Size
clang32	30/10/2021 18:09	File folder	
clang64	30/10/2021 18:09	File folder	
dev	30/10/2021 18:09	File folder	
etc	30/10/2021 18:10	File folder	
home	30/10/2021 18:09	File folder	
mingw32	30/10/2021 18:09	File folder	
mingw64	30/10/2021 18:09	File folder	
notepad++	30/10/2021 18:10	File folder	
opt	30/10/2021 18:09	File folder	
tmp	30/10/2021 18:09	File folder	
usr	30/10/2021 18:09	File folder	
var	30/10/2021 18:09	File folder	
cmdshell	30/10/2021 18:26	Windows Batch File	2 KB
fc_update	30/10/2021 18:26	Windows Batch File	1 KB
HG-ID	30/10/2021 18:26	File	1 KB
msys2	24/02/2020 12:57	Icon	26 KB
msys2_shell	24/02/2020 12:57	Windows Comma...	8 KB
octave	30/10/2021 18:26	VBScript Script File	3 KB
octave-firsttime	30/10/2021 18:26	VBScript Script File	3 KB
post-install	30/10/2021 18:26	Windows Batch File	2 KB
README	30/10/2021 18:26	Microsoft Edge H...	4 KB

Figure 7-1a Octave installed on Windows 10

Running Octave on Windows 10 requires double-clicking the indicated icon in Figure 7-1a. If Windows is your platform of choice, you can skip ahead to the "Using Octave" section and Figure

7-4. If on the other hand, your preferred platform is Linux/Ubuntu, then the following section is relevant.

On Ubuntu Linux, to install Octave, just click on the Ubuntu Software Center as illustrated in Figure 7-1.

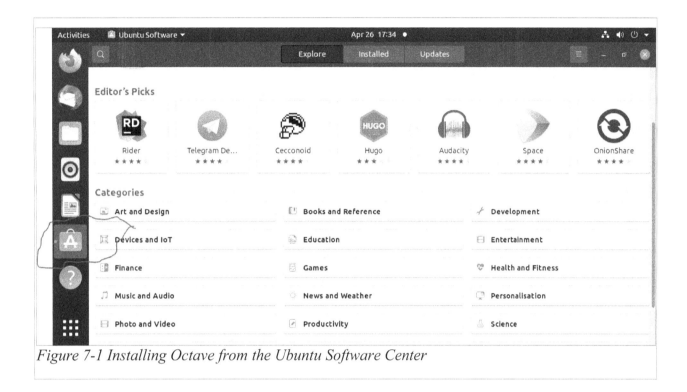

Figure 7-1 Installing Octave from the Ubuntu Software Center

Click the search button on the top left in Figure 7-1 and type in Octave.

Figure 7-2 Install the required Octave application

This should then display the available options as illustrated in Figure 7-2.

Select the required Octave application in Figure 7-2 and then click the Install button in Figure 7-3.

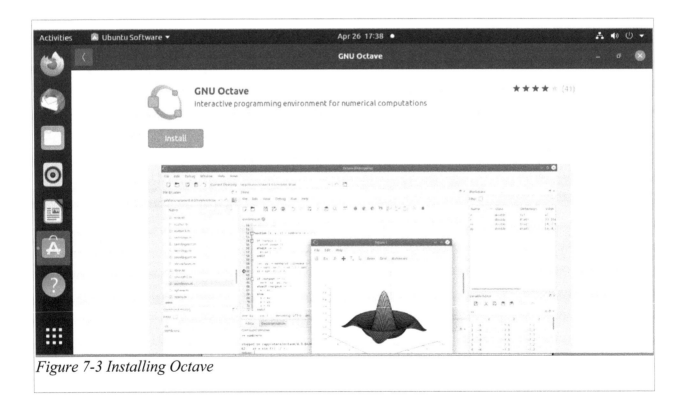

Figure 7-3 Installing Octave

Now that Octave is installed, let's take it for a test drive.

Using Octave

Figure 7-4 illustrates a really simple Octave interaction. In this case, we're using the graphical Octave setup and (in my particular environment, as noted above) it's installed in a Linux virtual machine running Ubuntu version 16.04.

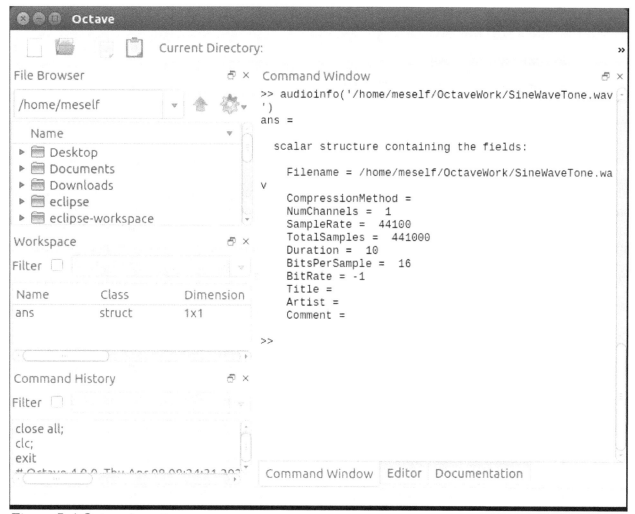

Figure 7-4 Octave in action

The important content for our immediate purposes in Figure 7-4 is in the command window (on the right hand side of the screen). In the command window, I run the *audioinfo* function on an input WAV file. This function allows you to read, write and retrieve information about a variety of audio file formats. Various audio file formats are supported including WAV, FLAC, and OGG Vorbis. In this case, we use WAV, which is what might be considered a de facto audio standard file format.

The *audioinfo* function is called by supplying the full path and file name, as follows:

info = audioinfo (filename)

In the case of Figure 7-4, the filename parameter is:

/home/meself/OctaveWork/SineWaveTone.wav

The result of the function call is a block of information about the audio file in question. In Figure 7-4, I supply a simple multi-tone WAV file called SineWaveTone.wav. The data returned by the call to audioinfo is a range of items including:

1. The number of channels (1)
2. The sample rate (44,100)
3. The total number of samples (441,000)
4. The signal duration (10 seconds)
5. The number of bits per sample (16)

This is all quite useful information and how might we go about confirming its correctness? Well, we just use our old friend Audacity to read in the WAV file and then have a look at the user interface as illustrated in Figure 7-5. In Figure 7-5, we can see the sample rate on the bottom left and the signal duration (in terms of samples) on the bottom right. The two values match the data returned from Octave, namely the project rate of 44100 samples per second and 441000 samples (duration).

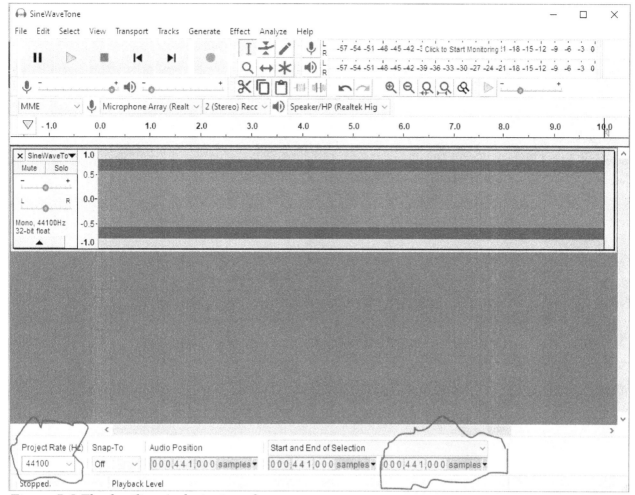

Figure 7-5 The familiar Audacity interface

From this, we can see that adding Octave to our DSP toolset provides us with yet another way to verify signal parameters. In passing, please note that in Figure 7-5 we used sample-based visualization. This can be changed to a number of different formats by clicking the dropdown control in the bottom right of Figure 7-5, as illustrated in Figure 7-6.

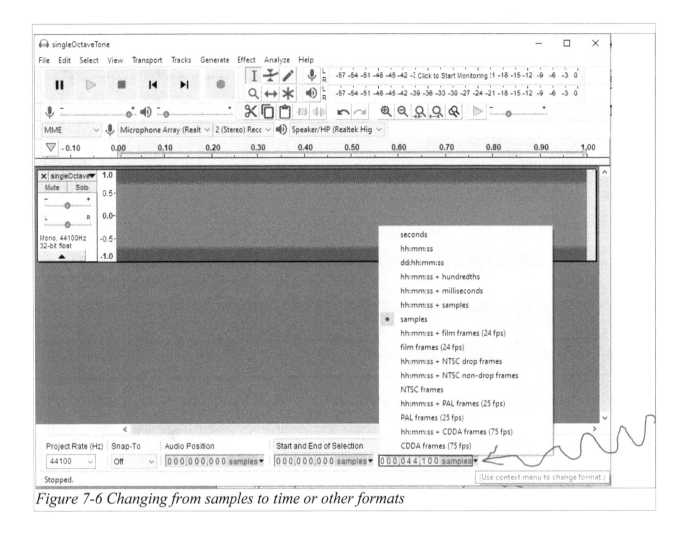

Figure 7-6 Changing from samples to time or other formats

Looking at Figure 7-6, we can change to use a time-based visualization if required, or any of the other types.

Viewing Audio Data In Octave

To look at the actual audio data inside a WAV file, the following command can be used:

audioread('/home/meself/SineWaveTone.wav')

Running this command in Octave results in Figure 7-7.

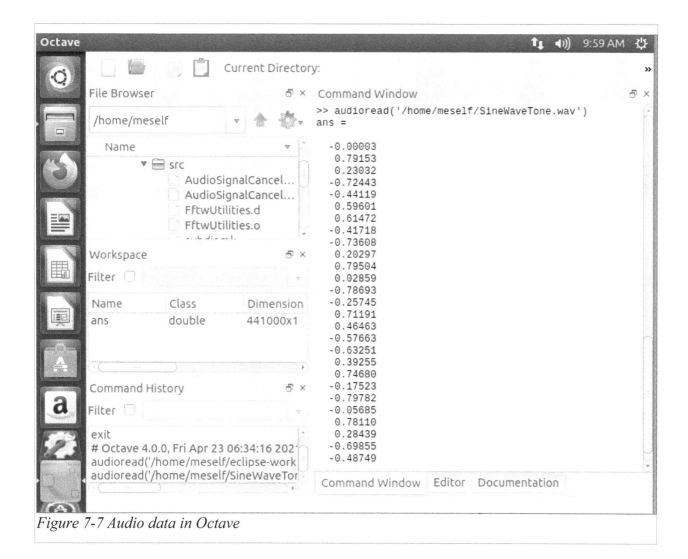

Figure 7-7 Audio data in Octave

So, the data in Figure 7-7 appears to follow a definite pattern. Excluding the first item (i.e., the value -0.00003), we see what looks like a repeating pattern of two positive values followed by two negative values. To visualise this data in graphical form we can, as usual, load the WAV file into Audacity and then zoom in (by repeatedly clicking View → Zoom) to produce the (zoomed-in) signal illustrated in Figure 7-8.

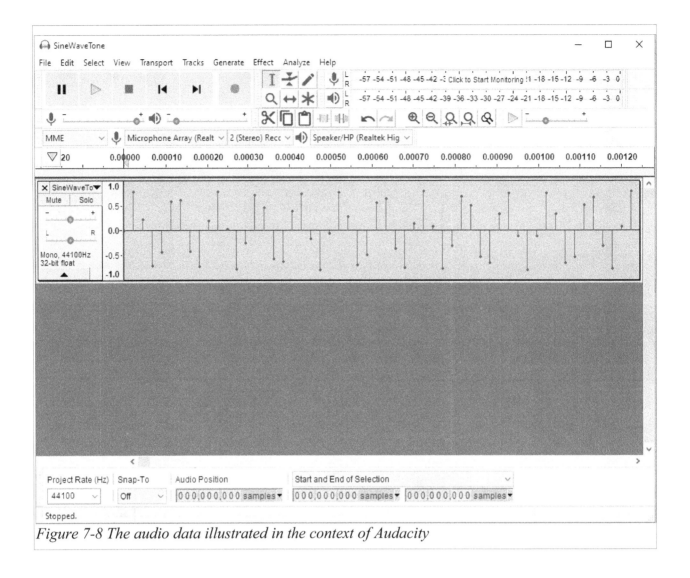

Figure 7-8 The audio data illustrated in the context of Audacity

Looking closely from left to right at Figure 7-8, you can now see that the pattern includes a number of blocks of 3 same-sign values interspersed with the blocks of 2 values. This might or might not be relevant for the DSP task at hand but it again illustrates the benefits of using a range of tools for signal review and analysis. It also shows that DSP development does involve an element of what might be called detective work.

Generating an Audio File in Octave

In the previous section, we saw how to examine an audio signal in Octave. What if we want to generate an audio signal in Octave? To do this, open the Octave command line interface as illustrated in Figure 7-9.

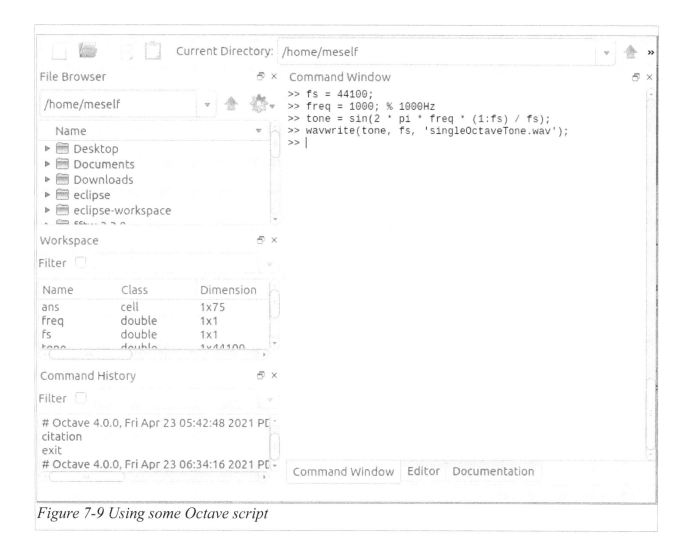

Figure 7-9 Using some Octave script

In Figure 7-9, we see some rather cryptic text on the top right hand side. Each of the four lines in Figure 7-9 goes together to create a WAV file with a single tone audio signal. Let's look at the script line by line. Note that the ">>" symbol in Figure 7-9 is the Octave cursor and doesn't need to be typed. Also, remember to end each line with a semicolon.

fs = 44100;

This line sets a variable to represent the sampling frequency

freq = 1000; % 1000Hz

This line sets the audio frequency for the signal. The percentage sign indicates a comment and is ignored by Octave.

tone = sin(2 * pi * freq * (1:fs) / fs);

This line is powerful! It generates a sinusoidal signal with frequency of 1000Hz and a duration of 1 second. The range is from 1 to fs or 1 to 44,100Hz and each value in the range is normalized, which is why division by fs is used.

wavwrite(tone, fs, 'singleOctaveTone.wav');

This is the line that creates the WAV file, called singleOctaveTone.wav.

What does the generated WAV file look like? Good question. As usual, let's import it into Audacity and have a look. One handy way to examine a WAV file in Audacity is to open the application and then drag the generated WAV file icon into the Audacity main screen. This produces the prompt in Figure 7-10.

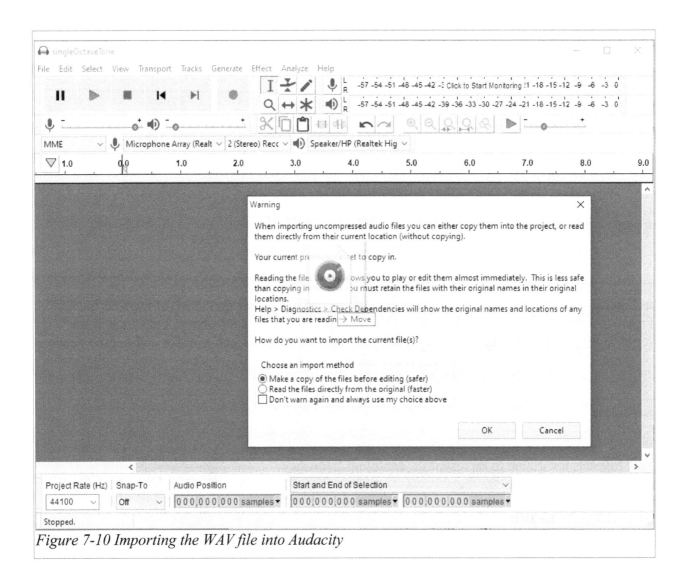

Figure 7-10 Importing the WAV file into Audacity

Just click OK and the WAV file signal is then displayed as illustrated in Figure 7-11. Please note, I've pressed View → Zoom a few times in order to display the sinusoidal form of the signal.

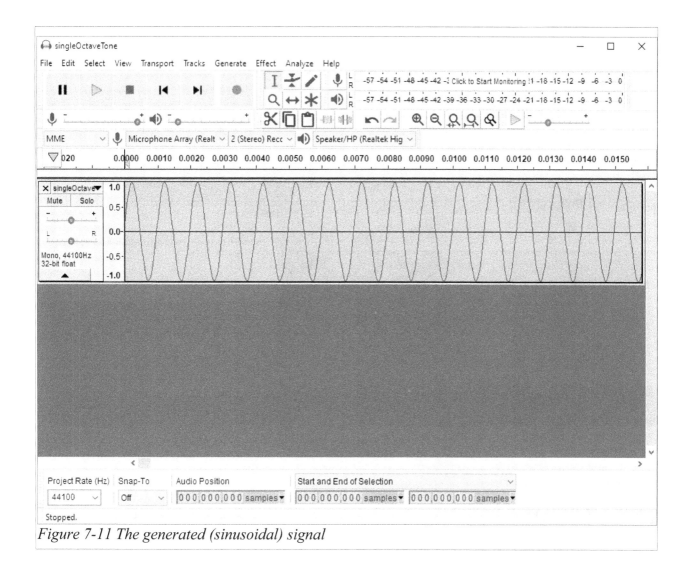

Figure 7-11 The generated (sinusoidal) signal

To determine the spectral content of the signal in Figure 7-11, we must select-all (on Windows, press Ctrl and the A key) of the signal and then select Analyse → Plot Spectrum...

If you forget to do the select-all operation, you'll see the warning in Figure 7-12.

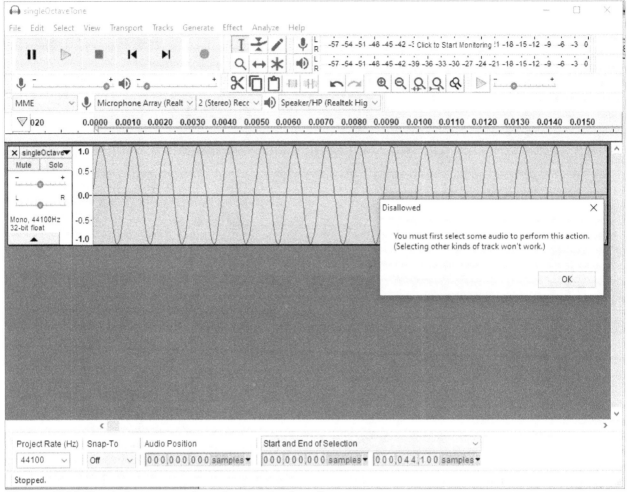

Figure 7-12 Don't forget to select the required audio

After clicking Select -> All, then select Analyse → Plot Spectrum... to produce the spectrum illustrated in Figure 7-13.

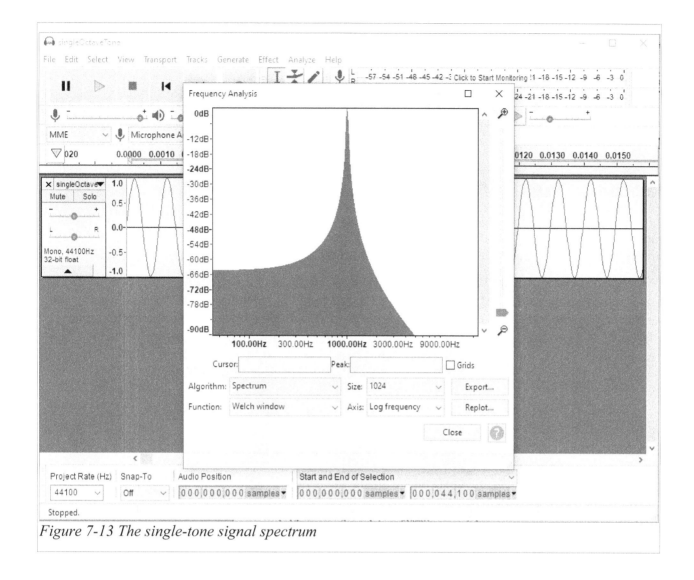

Figure 7-13 The single-tone signal spectrum

And finally, there we see the spectral peak that represents the single tone of 1000Hz as expected from the signal generated in Octave way back in Figure 7-9.

So, that's our whistlestop tour of GNU Octave. In fact, we've barely scratched the surface of what you can do with Octave. There are many additional facilities for DSP operations, such as, filtering and signal analysis. In the next chapter, we'll look a little more into Octave and see some interesting applications that are relevant to DSP.

Chapter 8 Looking a little more deeply into Octave

Octave DSP Uses – Finding Peak Values

Octave is a useful tool in its own right, i.e., it can be used in isolation from Audacity. The command line prompt in Octave provides access to a wide range of features. We've already seen some of these in the previous chapter where we looked at examining and originating audio data files.

Way back in Chapter 3, we briefly looked at the peak spectrum values that Audacity produces. This issue of peak detection is very important in DSP in general and Octave provides a neat way to extract such peak values. In the following script in Listing 1, we create a multi-tone time domain signal. This waveform is more complex than the ones we've looked at up to now and may be a little more typical of what might be encountered in the real world.

```
pkg load signal;

t = 2 * pi * linspace(0, 1, 1024);

# A complicated waveform

y = sin(3.141 * t) + 0.75 * cos(6.01 * t) + 0.11 * sin(8.10 * t + 1/5) + 0.1 *
sin(19.1 * t + 1/3);

data1 = abs(y); # Use positive values only

[pks idx] = findpeaks(data1);

data2 = y; # Double-sided

[pks2 idx2] = findpeaks(data2, "DoubleSided");

[pks3 idx3] = findpeaks(data2, "DoubleSided", "MinPeakHeight", 0.5);

subplot(1, 2, 1);

plot(t, data1, t(idx), data1(idx), 'xm');

axis tight;
```

Listing 1 Peak detection with Octave

After typing (or copying and pasting) the above into the Octave script command window, remember to press Enter after the last line. If all is well, you should then seen something like that illustrated in Figure 8.1. Please note that in Figure 8.1, I've added some hand drawn arrows to indicate the positions of the peak values. This is just in case your reader device doesn't render the peaks in a visible format.

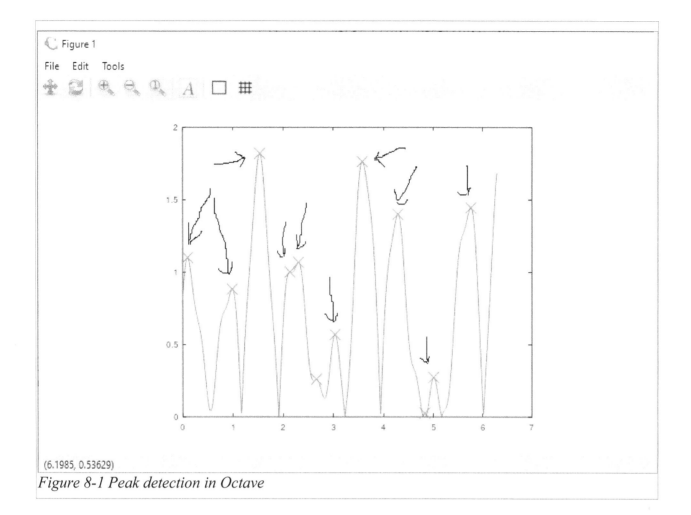

Figure 8-1 Peak detection in Octave

Notice the neat little x-marks (indicated by the arrow heads) on the peak values in Figure 8-1. On the 'live' Octave diagram, if you hover your mouse over the x-marks, you should see the actual numerical value at that point in the form of an (x, y) coordinate pair. One such sample value is illustrated in the bottom lefthand corner of Figure 8-1.

Another useful feature with Octave plots is to scale the diagram up or down by clicking one of the edges and dragging it in the appropriate direction.

Can Octave help us with digital filtering? Good question. Yes it can.

Using Octave to view a basic filter response

Let's say we want to see what a basic low pass filter output envelope looks like. The filter output we've seen so far using Audacity focuses only on the spectrum, i.e., the actual output values from the filter. In many of the examples we've seen so far, the spectrum has consisted of one or two peak values.

The frequency response envelope is different in that it illustrates the shape of the filter frequency response, i.e., what range of frequencies we expect to pass and what range we expect to be blocked. A picture is worth a thousand words. So, let's see what this looks like.

In fact amazingly, a low pass filter envelope can be produced using just two lines of script in the Octave command window. This is a further indication of the power and utility of Octave as illustrated in Listing 2.

```
pkg load signal;
freqz (fir1 (40, 0.3));
```

Listing 2 A low pass filter envelope

This two-line script generates a basic low pass filter and then displays the corresponding frequency response as illustrated in Figure 8-2.

Figure 8-2 also illustrates the phase response for the filter. Notice that the phase response is linear in the low pass frequency range. This linearity is a

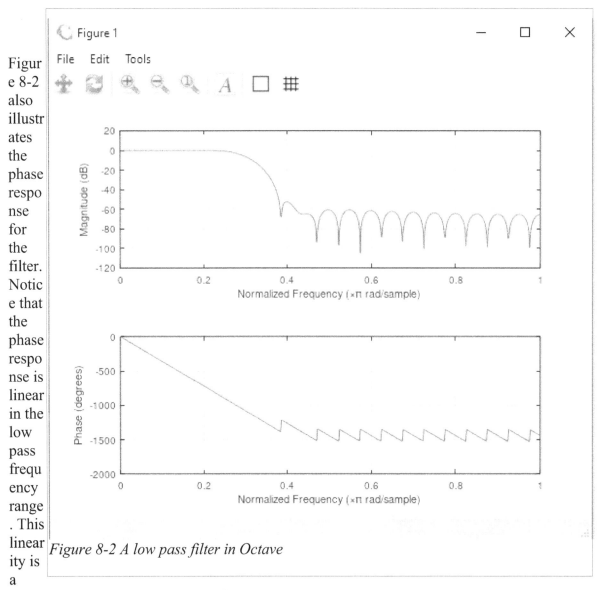

Figure 8-2 A low pass filter in Octave

desirable characteristic in such a filter.

Octave also supports other filter types, such as, band pass, high pass, band stop, and so on.

Basic Octave Sinusoidal Plot

The Octave examples we've looked at so far use generated signals. This is similar to the way we've used Audacity in the earlier examples where a synthetic signal is synthesized. As part of the DSP workflow, we may typically start with a simple signal and then build on this to create a more complex version. Getting started with Octave in this way is as simple as the following two lines in

Listing 3.

```
x = -10:0.1:10;
plot (x, sin (x));
```

Listing 3 A basic sinusoidal plot

The Listing 3 script produces the plot illustrated in Figure 8-3.

The waveform from Listing 3 can be added to in an arbitrary fashion the result can be plotted again and again as it becomes more complicated.

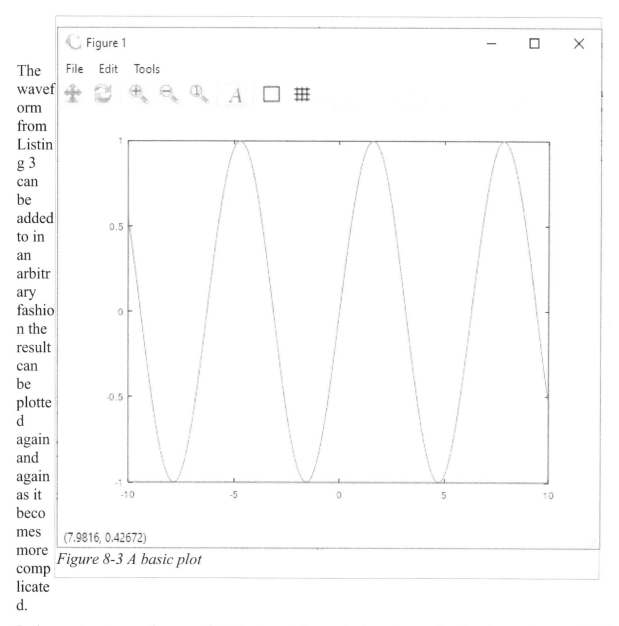

Figure 8-3 A basic plot

Let's now turn to another are of DSP where it is required to change the signal sample rate. This is a procedure called decimation.

Decimation Example

Imagine you have a signal with a higher than expected sample rate. An example might be an audio signal with a sample rate of 88.2kHz, which is twice the rate of audio CD. To reduce the sample rate to standard audio, we need to 'lose' half of the samples. This is termed downsampling the signal by a reduction factor of 2.

Zooming into our signal looks like Figure 8-4.

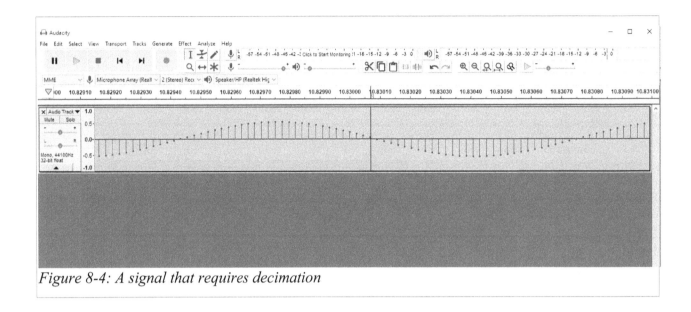

Figure 8-4: A signal that requires decimation

One question that arises is: To decimate the signal in Figure 8-4 by a factor of two, can't we just drop every second sample? Sadly, no. We must first filter the signal followed then by decimation. Otherwise, the straight (non-filtered) decimation will result in the introduction of unwanted artifacts into the new signal. It's important to understand why this occurs.

A low pass anti-aliasing filter is applied to the signal first. This removes those frequencies in the original signal that are above the Nyquist frequency of the processed signal. Without this step, the decimated signal would essentially be corrupted.

The Octave default (for the filter step) is an order n Chebyshev type I filter. If n is not specified, then the default is 8. After filtering we can then reduce the input sequence as required. Fortunately, Octave makes this all relatively straightforward as illustrated in Listing 4

```
pkg load signal;
t = 0:0.01:2;
x = chirp(t, 2,.5, 10,'quadratic') + sin(2 * pi * t * 0.4);
y = decimate(x, 2);    # Use a factor of 2 decimation
stem(t(1:121) * 1000, x(1:121),"-g;Original;");
hold on; # plot original
stem(t(1:4:121) * 1000, y(1:31),"-r;Decimated;");
hold off; # decimated
```
Listing 4 Filtering and decimating a signal

The script in Listing 4 produces the output in Figure 8-5.

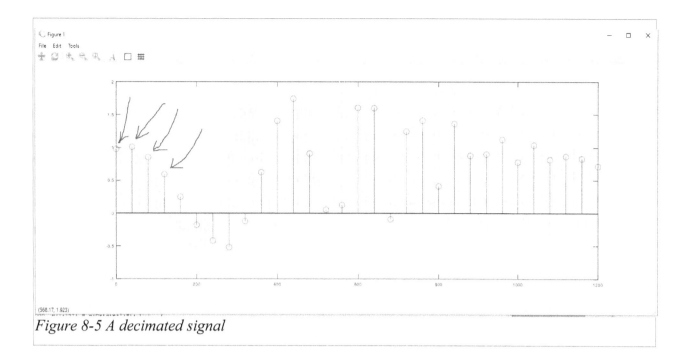

Figure 8-5 A decimated signal

Notice in Figure 8-5 the way the samples (in green) have been dropped. The arrowheads in Figure 8-5 point at the newly decimated signal samples. It's worth noting that the decimation process is not perfect as can be seen from those samples where there is a discrepancy with the original. This difference might or might not be important to your particular problem area. Again, this illustrates the need for an iterative DSP workflow.

In the next section, we look a little more at the original signal generated in Listing 4, a chirp signal.

A Chirp Signal

What does a chirp signal look like? Good question! A chirp signal uses a range of frequencies and looks like Figure 8-6 in the time domain.

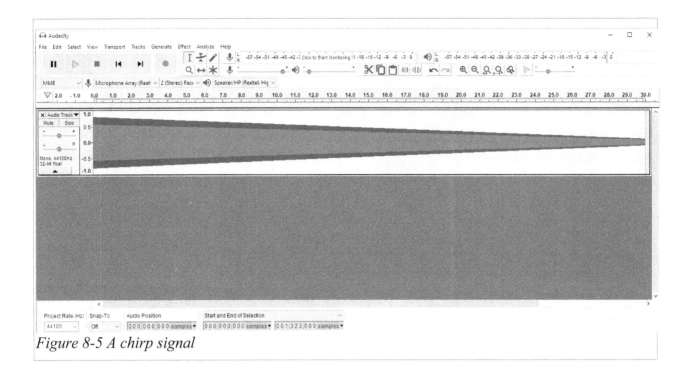

Figure 8-5 A chirp signal

A chirp signal can be played back and listened to; it has a rising sound as the signal sweeps through its constituent frequencies. In the frequency domain, a chirp looks like Figure 8-6.

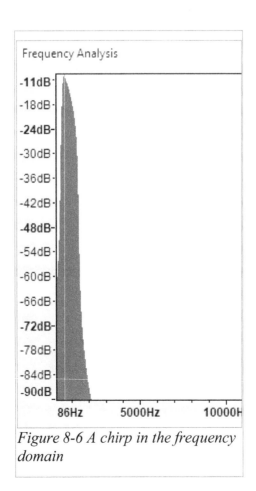

Figure 8-6 A chirp in the frequency domain

Notice the width of the peak in Figure 8-6. What is the origin of the frequency range in Figure 8-6? To answer this, look at the parameters used when generating the chirp signal as illustrated in Figure 8-7.

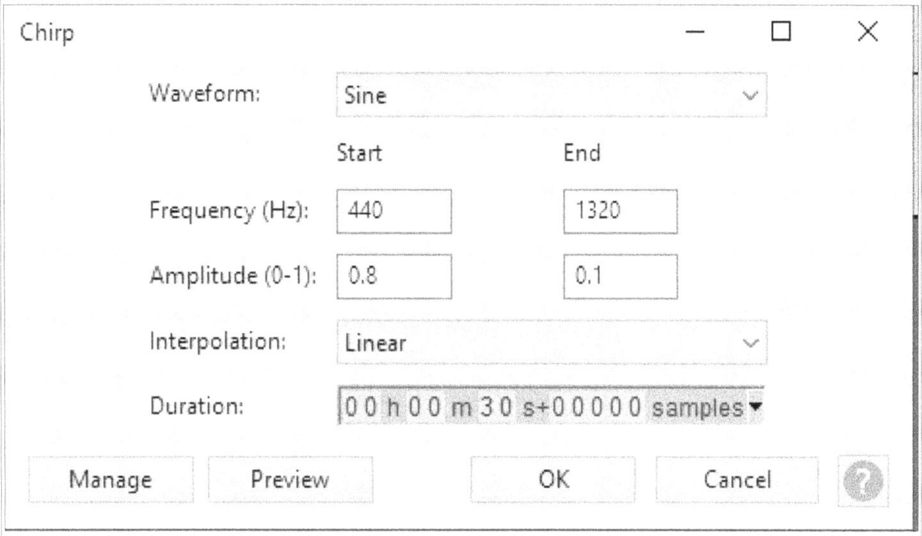

Figure 8-7 The chirp signal frequency selection

In Figure 8-7, the frequencies used in the chirp start at 440Hz and sweep through to 1320Hz. Notice the amplitude range from 0.8 down to 0.1This is why the signal sounds the way it does: rising in pitch as it plays back. It also explains why the spectrum is a wide peak comprised of a range of frequencies.

The next section looks at an interesting example of signal modulation and demodulation.

An Amplitude Modulation (AM) Example

AM is a technique used to transmit a message signal by way of a carrier wave. The amplitude of the carrier wave is varied in proportion to the message wave. This new wave is then transmitted across the medium and the process is reversed at the other end. AM is still used in radio transmission, though FM and other technologies provide improved fidelity. Wikipedia has a good article about AM.

In this section, we simulate AM using Octave as illustrated in Listing 5.

```
pkg load signal;
pkg load communications
Fs = 44100;
T  = 1; % Duration
Fc = 15000;
Fm = 10;
# Message and modulated signal
t = 0:1/Fs:T;
```

```
x = cos(5* pi * Fm * t);
y = ammod(x, Fc, Fs);
z = amdemod(y, Fc, Fs);
figure('Name','AM Modulation');
subplot(3, 1, 1); plot(t, x); title('Modulating (or message) signal');
subplot(3, 1, 2); plot(t, y); title('Modulated signal');
subplot(3, 1, 3); plot(t, z); title('Demodulated signal');
```
Listing 5 A simulated amplitude modulation example

In Listing 5, we have 3 waveforms (or signals):

1. A message wave
2. An amplitude-modulated wave carrier
3. A demodulated message wave

Running the script in Listing 5 produces Figure 8-8.

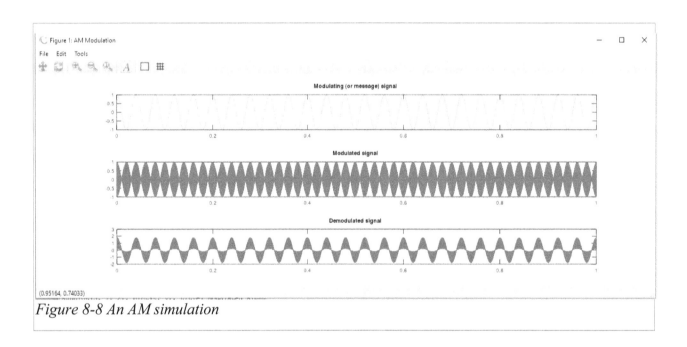

Figure 8-8 An AM simulation

In Figure 8-8, we simulate the creation of an AM wave and its transmission across some medium, followed by demodulation. The last step reduces the amplitude of the original signal but, its frequency content is unchanged. In other words, the signal survives the transmission process.

Let's now try to bring some of the main strands together and see how to use DSP tools to extract a signal from noise.

Extracting Signal Components Using the DFT

In this example, we start with a multi-tone signal, which is then additively mixed in with a noise signal. This way, the spectrum from each signal is joined up with the other. This is in fact a common use case in DSP and the challenge lies in removing the noise content and being left with the original multi-tone signal. Let's see how to do this.

```
Fs = 1500;              % Signal sample rate

T = 1 / Fs;             % Sampling period

L = 2000;               % Length of the signal

t = (0:L - 1) * T;      % Time axis value range
```

% Generate a composite signal that contains a 40 Hz sinusoid of amplitude 0.7 and a 90 Hz sinusoid of amplitude 1.0.

```
Signal = 0.7 * sin(2 * pi * 40 * t) + 1.0 * sin(2 * pi * 90 * t);

% Mix the signal with zero-mean white noise.


X = Signal + 2 * randn(size(t));


%Plot the modified signal in the time domain. Without spectrum analysis, it is
difficult to identify the frequency components by manual inspection of the
signal X.


plot(1000 * t(1:50), X(1:50))

title('Signal Mixed with Random Noise')

xlabel('Time (milliseconds)')

ylabel('X(t)')
```

Listing 6 A multi-tone signal mixed with noise

Figure 8-9 illustrates the composite signal.

Listing 7 illustrates the DFT which is used to generate the spectrum.

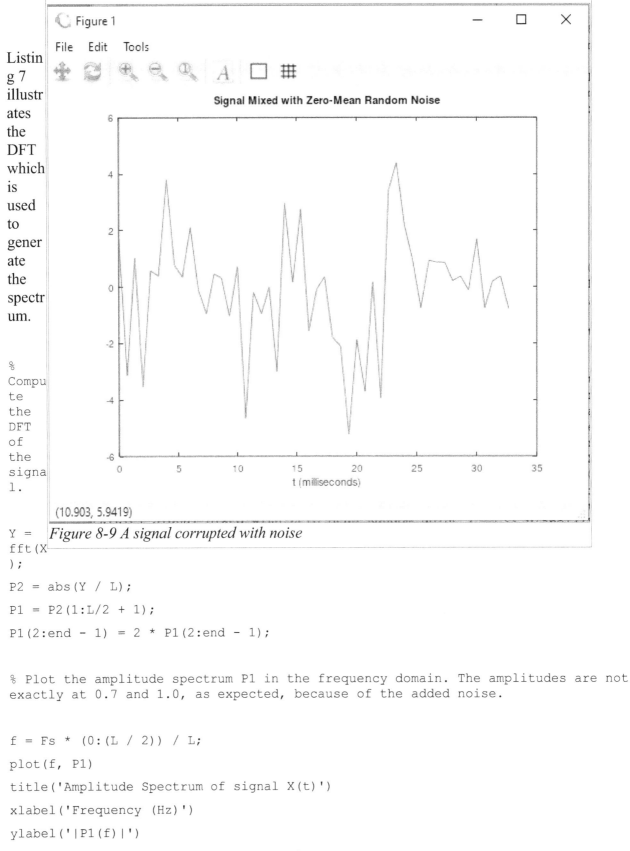

Figure 8-9 A signal corrupted with noise

% Compute the DFT of the signal.

```
Y = fft(X);
P2 = abs(Y / L);
P1 = P2(1:L/2 + 1);
P1(2:end - 1) = 2 * P1(2:end - 1);

% Plot the amplitude spectrum P1 in the frequency domain. The amplitudes are not
exactly at 0.7 and 1.0, as expected, because of the added noise.

f = Fs * (0:(L / 2)) / L;
plot(f, P1)
title('Amplitude Spectrum of signal X(t)')
xlabel('Frequency (Hz)')
ylabel('|P1(f)|')
```

Listing 7 The spectrum of the composite signal

Finally, in Figure 8-10, we see the spectrum.

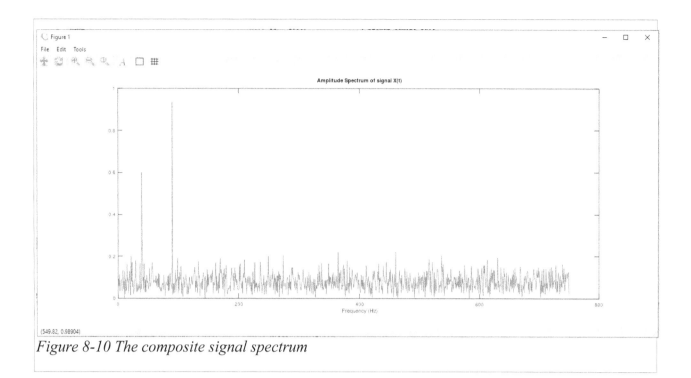

Figure 8-10 The composite signal spectrum

Notice in Figure 8-10, we see what looks like a minor miracle: The two peaks on the left hand side of the diagram. These two peaks represent the constituent frequencies from the original signal, i.e.,

```
Signal = 0.7 * sin(2 * pi * 40 * t) + 1.0 * sin(2 * pi * 90 * t);
```

The noise no longer affects the peaks when we see the frequency spectrum. This illustrates the power of the DFT.

Errors to watch out for when using Octave

In this section, I note in passing one common error that occurs when using Octave. Let's say we call one of the Octave functions, such as, the one for encoding amplitude modulation. You may see the accompanying error.

```
y = ammod(x,Fc,Fs);
error: 'ammod' undefined near line 1, column 1
```

```
The 'ammod' function belongs to the communications package from Octave
Forge which you have installed but not loaded.  To load the package, run
'pkg load communications' from the Octave prompt.
```

The fix for this is simple, and the corrected script is as follows:

pkg load communications

y = ammod(x,Fc,Fs);

The other common error is forgetting to press enter after the call to `ammod`.

Chapter 9 More Signal Analysis and a DIY Hearing Test

Digging into an Audio Signal as part of the DSP Process Pipeline

In this chapter, we'll look at some more benefits of using multiple perspectives when handling signals. Specifically, we'll look at a basic C++ program and compare it with the equivalent values from within Audacity.

A Pre-existing Audio File

Let's say we have a synthetically generated audio file. We've seen many of these in earlier chapters. Let's either generate the signal or load a pre-existing file into Audacity and zoom in a little (using View → Zoom → Zoom In, multiple times). Figure 9-1 illustrates the audio signal: it's just a basic single-tone signal. I've zoomed in enough times to reveal the sinusoidal contour of the signal.

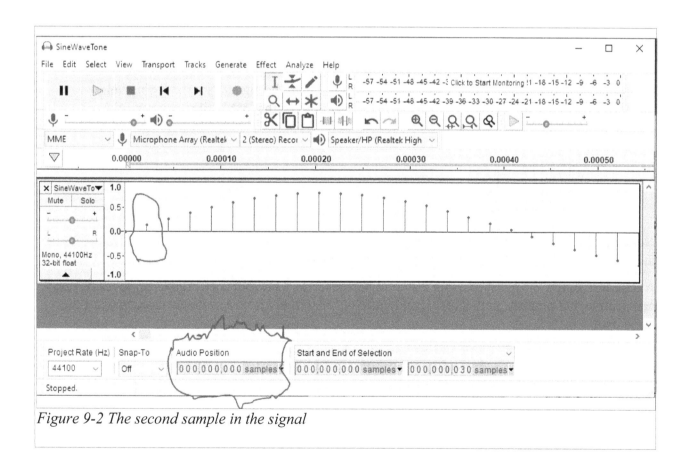

Figure 9-2 The second sample in the signal

By continuing to zoom into the signal, we eventually get to the point of seeing individual samples as illustrated below in Figure 9-2. Notice that I've marked one of the samples in the figure. We'll look at this sample more detail later.

Looking at the signal in the neighbourhood marked in Figure 9-2, we can now look at the three leftmost samples:

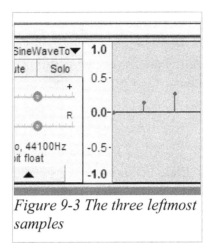

Figure 9-3 The three leftmost samples

In Figure 9-3, we have just three samples. Based on the vertical scale, the leftmost sample seems to have has the value zero, right? The second and third samples have values greater than zero and less than 0.5.

Using a C++ application, I extract the first four values from the signal. So, the listing below illustrates the first four signal values as they are read in from the WAV file.

```
Value of signal data[i] 0 0.000031
Value of signal data[i] 1 0.136047
Value of signal data[i] 2 0.268311
Value of signal data[i] 3 0.392517
```

Notice in the listing, that the WAV data tells a slightly different story from Audacity. Namely, that the first sample is in fact not zero. It has the value 0.000031.

Again, this shows the merit of using different perspectives. One tool (i.e., Audacity) gives us one perspective, but another, in this case, handcrafted C++ tool gives us a more accurate view of the same data.

Let's take the experiment a little further and include some more data (7 points) in the excerpt as illustrated in Figure 9-4.

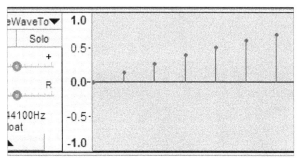

Figure 9-4 More data from the signal

What does the C++ program output for this figure look like? The following listing provides the details.

Value of signal data[i] 0 0.000031
Value of signal data[i] 1 0.136047
Value of signal data[i] 2 0.268311
Value of signal data[i] 3 0.392517
Value of signal data[i] 4 0.505493
Value of signal data[i] 5 0.603577
Value of signal data[i] 6 0.684082
More signal values

Notice in this listing that the last value is around the 0.684 mark. In practice, it may not be necessary to delve into such fine detail. But, as we've seen in earlier chapters, it's important to note that, with the right tooling, it is feasible to do so. Using multiple tools also facilitates the cross-checking of your signal data.

The C++ code snippet below illustrates the above signal data listing. The audioData parameter is simply an array of double values, created using a call to the libsndfile [3] audio library.

```
void dumpSignalData(double* audioData)
{
    for (int i = 0; i < 20; i++){
        printf("Value of signal data[i] %d %f\n", i, audioData[i]);
    }
}
```

The above code is, of course, just a simple for loop that examines the first 20 audio data array values, starting at element zero.

Exploring the Human Hearing Range

In this section, we'll look at an interesting aspect of Audacity – using it to explore the threshold of human hearing. In an earlier chapter, we saw a sidenote on the amazing hearing range of our canine companions.

Creating a Test Audio File

Audacity allows for the generation of a variety of test signals. If you click the Generate->Tone menu, it looks something like Figure 9-5:

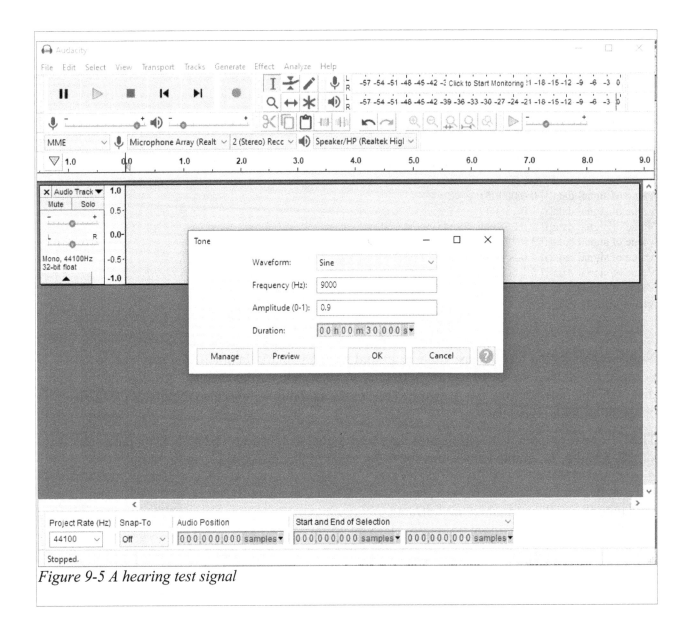

Figure 9-5 A hearing test signal

Make sure to select a frequency of interest that in the range of human hearing, i.e., between 20 Hz and 20 kHz [4].

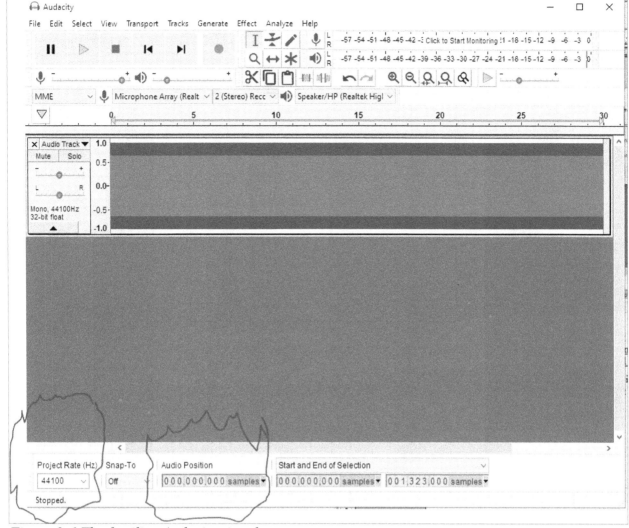

Figure 9-6 The familiar Audacity signal

In the diagram, I've used a 9000Hz sine-based waveform. Click OK to generate the signal and you'll see the familiar Audacity blue block in Figure 9-6.

As usual, notice in the bottom left of Figure 9-6, the sample rate (highlighted) is the default value of 44,100 Hz and the position of the audio position (or signal cursor is zero), i.e., the leftmost sample.

Spectrum Analysis

So, we now have a basic single-tone (9000 Hz) audio signal. To verify that the signal contains the required 9000 Hz tone, let's do the familiar spectrum analysis, by clicking Analyze->Plot Spectrum... to produce Figure 9-7.

Notice in Figure 9-7 the single peak of 9000 Hz generated using the default Audacity settings.

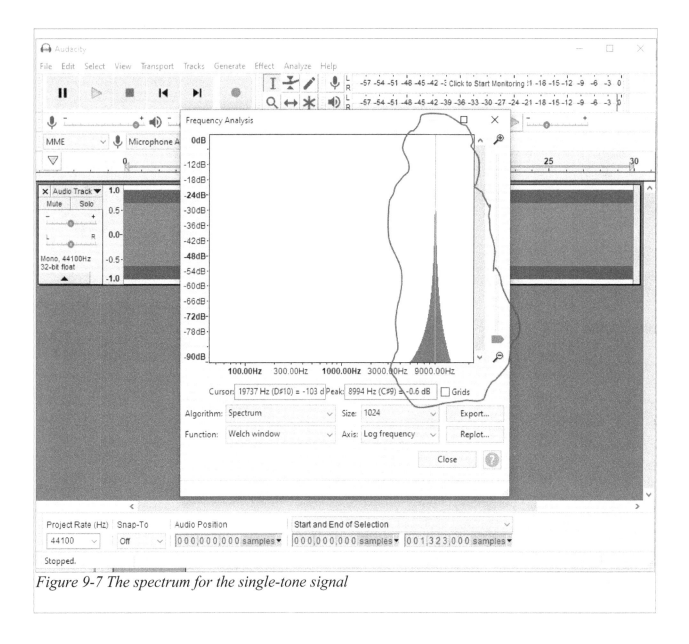

Figure 9-7 The spectrum for the single-tone signal

So, what does such a signal in Figure 9-7 sound like? Well, as mentioned in an earlier chapter, Audacity provides a playback option. As a precaution, make sure that your machine sound volume is set low – single tone signals sound pretty horrible. As soon as your volume is set low, hit the green play button as illustrated in Figure 9-8:

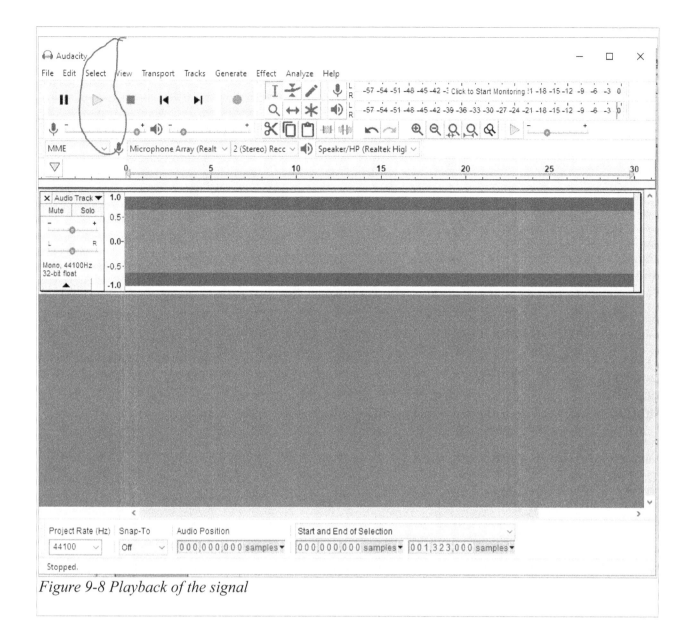

Figure 9-8 Playback of the signal

You can then play around with generating other signals with higher/lower frequencies. This is then a really basic hearing test.

Conclusions

While DSP is a mathematical discipline, the practical aspects of it can be readily understood. This is particularly the case when using modern software tools, such as, Audacity and Octave. These products provide many features for signal creation, visualization, filtering, playback, and so on. Octave can also be integrated into high level languages, such as, C++. In this context, Octave becomes a powerful engine that is driven by end user source code.

As we've seen, digital signals exist as sequences of numbers and it is useful and instructive to delve into these values. As in any technical discipline, it is useful to have a roadmap. DSP is no exception and for this reason, we use a simple workflow-based pipeline. Changing perspective on your signals is a crucial element of such a workflow-based approach. This also helps avoid going down blind alleys, such as, modifying an audio signal and then forgetting to listen back to the changes. It is not unknown for a bug in an algorithm to have completely garbled the audio.

A range of very useful and user-friendly free software tools is available online and this helps a lot in getting to grips with the subject. The DSP tools allow for moving back and forth between the time and frequency domains. For the case of audio DSP, the simple act of listening to a signal playback in Audacity can help in determining the quality of that signal. This is particularly useful when your work involves modifying the signal.

I hope the book has helped a little in demystifying the subject. I wish you the best of luck in your DSP endeavors!

Further material is of course available online and do feel free to look at my blog on dsprelated.com [5].

Further Reading

[1]   Understanding Digital Signal Processing 3rd Edition by Richard G. Lyons

[2]   GNU Octave User Manual - https://octave.org/doc/v6.2.0/

[3]   http://www.mega-nerd.com/libsndfile/

[4]
        https://www.ncbi.nlm.nih.gov/books/NBK10924/#:~:text=Humans%20can%20detect%20so
unds%20in,to%2015%E2%80%9317%20kHz.

[5]   My blog: https://www.dsprelated.com/blogs-
1/nf/Stephen_Morris.php?searchfor=stephen+morris&year=

Index

Alphabetical Index

adjacent analysis frequencies 45
analogue domain..18
analysis frequencies...48
Audacity 13
audio editor..13
continuous signals 11
digital signal 15
Digital signal processing 7
Discrete Fourier Transform 38
disk space...29
DSP process..34
filtering 29
fractal context 11
Hamming window function 42
Hanning 42
leaks 44
listening 30
logarithmic scale..42
Mathematics, physics and computing..7
narrowly defined peaks..44
Nyquist frequency 12
peak value..25
period..19
Plot Spectrum 22
Plotting the spectrum 25
quantization error...18
quantized and digitized samples 12
Samples...27
sampling and quantization..12
shifts of perspective 52
signal...10
signal discontinuities 42
sinusoidal..30
sinusoidal wave pattern 16
smoothing 42
time domain 7
WAV..19
zero crossings 20